Extraordinary Women - The Things They Have Done, That You Never Knew

By

Chaz Allen

ISBN: 1-4140-1745-6 (e-book)
ISBN: 1-4140-1746-4 (Paperback)

This book is printed on acid free paper.

1stBooks — rev. 10/29/03

Radio Teeth

Californians were a little paranoid. Some may not think that's so unusual, but this time they had a reason. After all, a Japanese submarine had been spotted off the Santa Barbara coast and someone had seen a Zero flying near Santa Monica. Japanese-Americans had been sent to interment camps at Manzanar and everyone was suspicious of everyone else. One particular California woman had double reason to be nervous. Not only did she worry about the Japanese, but she had an appointment with her dentist, and she hated the dentist. But even in the middle of a war life must go on, even for someone with bad teeth. And she did have awful teeth. What's worse, her job required her to have a great smile, so teeth were important. She spent the better part of the day in the dentist's chair getting her teeth drilled, both uppers and lowers, and temporary fillings made of lead were put in while the dentist finished the permanent ones. Yes, lead. That's what fillings were made out of in those days. A few nights later while driving back to her ranch after work, she heard music. She even recognized the song, and she reached down to turn off the radio, but the radio wasn't on. The music got louder and she noticed her mouth vibrating with the rhythm of the music. Then, as quickly as it came, the music faded out. Fairly sure she was going crazy, she hesitated to tell anyone about it, but the next day she decided to trust someone and she mentioned it to her very good friend Buster. He asked her if she was at the intersection of Moorpark and Coldwater and if she had any lead fillings. Well, needless to say, she was amazed. But he only laughed and told her that another friend of his had picked up the radio station near Moorpark and Coldwater through the fillings in his teeth. She was intrigued and she started driving around trying to pick up the station again, but with no luck. She had just about forgotten about the whole episode when one night in a totally different location, she picked up not music, but morse code. Can you imagine? Her mouth started jumping, with de-de-de-de bouncing off her molars. The next day she told the authorities and they called in the FBI. Sure enough, the authorities ferreted out a secret underground Japanese radio station in someone's basement. It turned out that their gardener was a spy. It sounds more like a zany plot of an "I Love Lucy" episode, but it's true. What happened to that California woman who hated going to the dentist? Well, she really never lost the fear of the dentist, but she did go on to become known and loved for so many other things, like "I Love Lucy!" ***It's a Little Known Fact*** that Lucille Ball's bad teeth may have influenced the outcome of World War II. And the friend who told her she wasn't crazy? Well, that was Buster Keaton.

Cousin Caroline

At one time or another, you've probably heard of John Jacob Astor. His story's a good one, and you might even say that it's a real life rags to riches American dream come true. John Jacob was the son of a poor German butcher. When he sailed to America in 1783, he didn't have a penny to his name and could barely speak English, but that never slowed him down. John sold musical instruments, dabbled in real estate, and cornered the fur trade in America. When he died, he was the richest man in the country. John had a handful of children and they inherited all those riches. Within a generation or two the Astor family had set itself up as reigning royalty in New York's high society. The queen of that era was Caroline Astor. Anyone who wanted to break into the ranks of New York's elite had to stay in her good graces. In her black wig and strings of priceless jewels, she counted herself the supreme judge of social acceptability, and there wasn't anyone who'd dare question her authority. If she said you were in, well you were, but if she kept you out, that's more than likely where you stayed. In the 1880's, Caroline and the rest of the Astors had been wealthy for three generations and they frowned on new money, or anyone who had made their riches by working for it. Like the English aristocracy they mimicked, the New York "old guard" excluded anyone who was in "trade." And that included the Vanderbilts, who had made their money in railroads. For years, Caroline had refused to acknowledge the Vanderbilt family, which claimed even more wealth than the Astors. They were kept on the outskirts of society. The invitations to the big Astor parties never came. Finally the Vanderbilts had enough. They began to throw lavish balls and house parties of their own, and they in turn left the Astors off the invitation list. It was a new kind of family feud, and it was fought long and hard inside the mansions of New York society. For quite a while there was no clear winner, and then the Vanderbilts offered 30,000 dollars for a season box at the Academy of Music Opera House and they were turned down flat. It seemed that particular opera house was heavily supported by the Astors. It was the last straw for William Henry Vanderbilt. *It's a Little Known Fact* that the head of the Vanderbilt family was so mad that he got together a syndicate of the rich and resolved to build an opera house where they could have all the private boxes they wanted. And even if you're not a lover of opera, you probably know of it. After all, it was New York's original Metropolitan Opera House, the beacon, some might say, of high society.

The Politician

He wanted to run for public office, and like most people running for office, Bill Canby knew that it would take something special to get the voter's attention. He was sure that he had the perfect thing to do it. Bill was a historian by profession. He made a study of history and reported what he found to the public in general and to the school that employed him, of course. But deep down he had an ambition to be in public office, and he was sure that he would be a good politician if he could just get in office. But in 1870, historians weren't held in that high of a regard and he knew that it would take some kind of gimmick to get the voters to notice him, much less elect him. Bill did have an Ace in the Hole. He was the grandson of famed seamstress Betsy Ross. So, Bill decided that he would play his ace card. During a visit to Washington he went before the Congress of the United States and made a speech, one that he was sure would make all the newspapers and get him noticed-maybe even elected. He told the heartwarming story of how his grandfather George Ross, along with George Washington and Robert Morris, were on the committee to design a new flag for the new country. He told of how the committee went to his seamstress grandmother Betsy Ross, who re-designed their rough sketch and came up with the now famous Stars and Stripes. Bill got his wish, for the most part anyway. His speech was written down in the Congressional record and made public. Bill did get a lot of attention for his speech and his famous and heroic grandparents. There was just one little problem with Bill's plan. It wasn't true! Bill made the whole thing up. Betsy Ross never touched the flag, and neither did his grandfather George, Robert Morris or George Washington. ***It's a Little Known Fact*** that the original flag of 13 stars representing the original 13 colonies with red and white stripes was designed by Mr. Francis Hopkinson in 1777, nine years after Betsy supposedly created it. Frank was a Navy flag maker. He had made hundreds of flags in his life and he was the one who designed and sewed Old Glory. So why has Betsy always been given the credit? Well, because of the speech that her grandson Bill made in Congress. It went into the Congressional record and was republished by almost every newspaper in the country. It didn't help Bill though. He lost the election anyway. Frank was never paid by the government for making the flag, so he must still own the rights to it!

Margaret's Arthritis

Sometimes you just have to slow down and smell the honeysuckle. And you must to get the full flavor of the story of Margaret Marsh. This story took place in the deep South at the beginning of the last century. Margaret's mother Mary Isabelle, called Belle in true Southern fashion, was very outspoken about women's rights and would take her young daughter to suffragette rallies. May Belle founded the more liberal wing of the suffragette movement that became the League of Women Voters. What a scene of conflict and tension that must have been for young Margaret. Women parading around in the streets were laughed at by most men everywhere in America, but no where more so than in the deep South where a proper woman was supposed to know her place -and stay there. It must have taken some nerve and courage for Margaret's mother to defy the polite society of the day. It took what Margaret would later call gumption.

Inspired by her mother, young Margaret did whatever she thought was the right thing to do. She thought it was right to volunteer to help in the hospital wards reserved for the poor. The fact that they were the wards of the poor black people was just unacceptable to the fancy ladies in town who refused Margaret membership in the Junior League. Margaret took her independence and gumption to her job as the first woman to cover hard news for the biggest paper in town. Just as she was becoming quite a well-known journalist and making a name for herself, a debilitating case of arthritis in her ankles and feet made it impossible for her to cover the stories she loved to write. The doctors sent her home to bed. Her husband John Marsh eventually tired of lugging home dozens of books from the library for her to read, so one day he brought home a portable typewriter instead and said that since she had now read every book in the library, the only thing for her to do was to write her own story. Which she did. ***It's a Little Known Fact*** that a bad case of arthritis sent Margaret Marsh home to her bed where she eventually wrote, using her maiden name Margaret Mitchell, one of America's great novels: Gone with the Wind.

Lost Woman

The year was 1850, and it was in October in the Nebraska territories that a group of travelers boarded a stage coach for the three week trip to the Oregon territory. The three men and one woman were engaged in friendly chat, when a couple of hours into the trip the coach slowed to a stopped. There on the side of the road was an old Indian woman. Passenger B.J. Cummings remembers the first time he saw her. Cummings was a banker headed west to open a new bank, and he wrote in his diary that the "lost woman" was very spry. That's how the driver greeter her, by the name of Lost Woman." She got into the coach comfortably, as if she had done it a dozen times, and indeed she had. She was a regular on the line, traveling back and forth across much of the Dakota and Nebraska territories. Whether or not the other passengers minded her being there, a few miles down the road she would prove herself to be indispensable.

The stage hadn't gone very far when the driver pulled up short again. Three armed men on horseback stood blocking the road. All the passengers were ordered out of the stage, robbed and left on the side of the road. The bandits took off with their money, their valuables and the stage coach. They were 30 miles from nearest stage depot. Ginny Long didn't think she could make the walk, much less be able to dodge the bandits, hostile Indians, and other scoundrels they might encounter along the way. They had no food, no water and no shelter. Lost Woman told the passengers to stay where they were and that she would be back with help soon. She left and the other passengers were sure they had seen the last of her. When the second day broke and Lost Woman had still not returned, they started estimating their chances of making it on their own. Just about the time that they had decided to try walking to the next stop, Lost Woman returned with about 10 other Indians, fresh horses, food and water. They were taken to the next stage depot and sent on their way. They thanked Lost Woman for literally saving their lives. But it wasn't until they heard one of the other Indians address her in her language that they realized who she was, and that saving lives was nothing new to this special woman. *It's a Little Known Fact* that Lost Woman had preformed similar feats of heroism most of her life. Nearly 45 years earlier, she had done the same thing for the very first group of white men to ever come through the area: the famed scouting and mapping mission of Merriweather Lewis and William Clark. The woman who was now called Lost Woman was none other than Sacajawea herself.

The Tomboy

Millie was a tomboy and everyone in town knew it! From the time she was able to walk, she was always doing things that usually just the boys did. She was as rough and tumble as they come. She was born in her grandparents' home in Kansas in 1897, and for the most part she and her kid sister Pidge lived a pretty privileged life thanks to her grandpa Alfred's position in the community. Millie had a flair for the extraordinary, often choosing activities like skateboarding over high brow social affairs. That's right, Millie built one of the first skateboards. It's not a recent invention. In fact, she and Pidge created a contraption similar to a stunt ramp, which of course Millie would fly down on a skateboard, scaring both her grandpa and grandma. The girls were eventually reunited with their father Edwin in Des Moines, Iowa, where he had taken an executive position with the Rock Island Line Railroad. Grandpa Alfred disapproved, even after Edwin was promoted and was able to provide the girls with a much improved standard of living. But Millie, only ten years old at the time, was happy to be with her dad. However, this happy time was very somewhat short-lived. Millie's father began to drink heavily, and was eventually fired from his job with the railroad, not only casting shame and financial hardship on the family but also subjecting the girls to local gossip. So, at the age of seventeen, Millie left home to live with friends in Chicago. Her mother's trust fund provided her with income and allowed her to attend private schools. While visiting Pidge at a college prep school in Canada, Millie decided to train as a nurses aid in Toronto. She then served as a voluntary aid detachment nurse at a military hospital until the Armistice in November 1918. Millie was fascinated with her work and the following fall enrolled as a medical student at Columbia University. She did extremely well in her studies, and she was well on her way to becoming one of the first women medical doctors in America. But you'll remember that Millie was something of a tomboy, and medicine was just not going to satisfy that restlessness she had in her soul. On a trip to California to visit her father she attended an aerial meet at Daugherty Field in Long Beach. When she was offered the chance to don a helmet and goggles and go for a ride in an airplane, and that was the end of medical school. *It's a Little Known Fact* that the woman who's name became synonymous with aviation and the first woman to fly solo across the Atlantic in 1932, was suppose to be a doctor …Amelia Earhart.

Mary Goes To New York

Can you imagine how Mary Anderson felt? She was a proper Southern lady of Alabama visiting New York City for the first time. It was cold, oh, so cold in New York in the winter of 1903. Mary was visiting the big city as a tourist. Of course at that time, cameras were about the size of a table and folks weren't prone to carrying them around, so Mary brought her sketch pad. She was going to do a little sketching of the tall buildings and then show them to her friends back home and tell them about the big city way up North. The buildings must have seemed magnificent to a lady who had come all the way from Alabama, and Mary must have had a busy pencil. She had the ambition to go anywhere and everywhere. But she hadn't counted on the cold northern winters. In Alabama they had a little winter, but nothing like what she faced in New York City. She though she was ready for snow, but she didn't know how cold it would make her fingers, or how her nose would run, or how cold her feet would be -oh her feet were cold. And unlike Alabama, the cold didn't go away. It lasted months. Her friends had told her that the best way to get around the big city was by the streetcar. So Mary Anderson traveled by streetcar and wrote in her journal that she was most admiring of the streetcar drivers, how skilled, kind and courteous they were of a lady. Mary was a tenderhearted soul who didn't like to see people having a hard time. So Mary was upset for the streetcar drivers when she saw them having such a terrible time with the snow and ice. They were constantly having to stop the streetcar, get out, run up front and do adjusting. When they came back into the warm car Mary could see that their hands were nearly frozen blue each time. Then she had an idea. She whipped out her sketch pad and started drawing a device she figured would help those poor motormen. It would let them drive the streetcars without ever having to get out of them because of bad weather. She sketched a spring-loaded swinging arm with a rubber blade on the outside of the windshield that could be moved back and forth by a hand lever inside the cab. Her friends teased her about it, but Mary was determined to patent her invention, which she did in 1904. *It's a Little Known Fact* that Mary Anderson, a Southern belle who felt sorry for some cold but kindly street car drivers, invented the windshield wiper. And by 1913 her little sympathetic invention had become standard equipment on every automobile made.

Friends in High Places

Have you ever heard of a group of business men who took over an entire country? It happened and it happened very close to home. In 1893 a group of American businessmen in Hawaii formed a political coalition and overthrew the legitimate Hawaiian government. After they seized power and jailed the King and Queen of Hawaii, they sent a delegation to Washington, D.C. to ask the President and Congress to quickly annex Hawaii as a territory and make it a state. They must have thought that they would have this island paradise all to themselves. But there was a problem, and that was 17 year old Princess Lalulani. With her mother and father in jail and her native island being taken away from her people, she knew it was up to her to do something. So went right to the source. She traveled to Washington to plead the case of her people. Needless to say, she was pretty nervous about the ordeal. After all, this was Congress and the White

House. But two of her best friends told her that she would do fine. One offered to go with her. She had spent more time in the last year with these two friends than any one else, and if they said she could do it, then she believed it too. Well, she went and presented her case. She told how unscrupulous businessmen had taken over nearly every aspect of the political and financial affairs of her native Hawaii. She told how her people were being exploited and losing their property that had been in families for hundreds of years. The young woman was so well spoken, so well versed in American customs, manners and courtesies that she impressed everyone she met. She was a brilliant conversationalist and she definitely had the ear of Capital Hill. Not only was she passionate, but savvy, and she literally talked circles around the people sent by the businessmen to undermine her. How was it that she was able to be such an outstanding spokesperson of her people? Who was it that had taught her so well? Well, she did have the two very special friends, two men who thought the world of the young beauty from Hawaii and spent over a year teaching her the skills she would need. She couldn't have had better teachers. ***It's a Little Known Fact*** that Princess Kalulani was the private and personal student of two men vacationing in Hawaii who took on the tasks of teaching the young princess at the request of her father: Mr. Robert Lewis Stevenson and Mr. Mark Twain.

Good Morning To All

Mildred and Patty were more than just sisters. They were colleagues as well, and they loved their work. In the late 1800's, Mildred was teaching kindergarten in the same experimental school in Louisville, Kentucky where Patty was principal. Mildred, a real lover of music, thought it would be great to write a song for the children at the school. An expert in spiritual songs and an accomplished organist, Mildred thought she could pool her talents with Patty's expertise in kindergarten education to create a wonderful song. And so they did. The jingle was eventually entitled, "Good Morning to All", and was a hit with the kids, which just tickled the sisters pink. In 1893, they published their work in a collection called "Song Stories of Kindergarten." The sisters were proud of that little song book, and went happily back to their school duties believing they had written a song that children would sing forever. And they did! But

25

not like they had planned. Little did they know that their heartfelt efforts would one day be clouded by a rather sour turn of events. In 1924, thirty-one years after the sisters published their song, Patty was head of the department of kindergarten education at Columbia University's Teacher College when a man by the name of Robert Coleman decided that he really liked "Good Morning to All". He liked it so much, in fact, that he decided to publish the song without asking the sister's permission. Then, to add insult to injury, Coleman had the audacity to add a second verse to the song, again without the consent of the original composers. Finally, as if that wasn't bad enough, the new verse that was added popularized the song so much that in time Mildred and Patty's original verse was all but forgotten. Suddenly their little kindergarten diddy was being sung at parties and gatherings all over the country. It was very popular indeed! Needless to say, when the sisters caught wind of the whole mess, they were less than amused. Mildred died in 1916, but Patty wasn't about to let the insult go unchallenged.

She took Mr. Coleman to court and, much to his disgrace, proved that she and Mildred did indeed own the original melody. *It is a Little Known Fact* that the verse Mr. Coleman added to the song which was originally written as "Good Morning to All", became probably the most popular and familiar song in the world today, sung by children and adults alike at a very special occasion. Because of the lawsuit which Patty Hill brought nearly a century ago, her family is still entitled to royalties whenever *"Happy birthday to you"* is used for commercial purposes.

Katie's Poem

Yes, this was it, exactly what Katie was looking for. Inspiration! Here she was indeed inspired. Katie had just reached the summit of Pike's Peak, fourteen thousand feet up. She took a good look around and she knew. Katie was a professor at a small college back East, and frankly, she'd gotten sick of it. All she ever wrote were literary critics, a few travel guides, that sort of thing. So she'd decided to take the summer off and go to Colorado. She convinced some other teachers to hike with her up to the top of Pike's Peak, and here she was. She looked around, and the beauty of the scene took her breath away with its snow-capped mountains and the green valley below. Here she felt inspired to write something that she would be proud of. She took out her little notebook and scribbled down the first few lines that came into her head. When she showed the poem to her fellow teachers, they were all shocked. "This is awful!" they said. "What kind of junk is this?" They went so far as to tell Katie to destroy the words she'd written, for if anyone ever saw the poem, her academic career would be finished. They called it trite and silly. How could she ever expect to be taken seriously again? But Katie was proud of what she'd written, and not only did she not destroy it, she added to it. She started to see other things that inspired her. It was as if something on Pike's Peak woke her up so she could see the world around her. She added more verses to her little poem. She showed it to a few friends again, and again they told her not to let anyone see it. On top of all the criticism, everyone was up in arms over a single word in the poem. One word! But Katie stuck to her guns. She knew that she had to share what she'd written, so she submitted it for publication. And like the teachers, one publisher after another rejected it. But one tiny church near her hometown heard of the poem and wanted it for their newsletter. They even paid her $25. But when some of her fellow professors at the college saw it, they took her to task! Poor Katie had finally been inspired to write words she truly believed, and now she was criticized from coast to coast, and all for the use of one word. A few of her critics even told her she might get away with it if she changed that word. It just didn't fit, it just didn't make sense. But Katie thought about how she'd stood on top of Pike's Peak, and the magnificent view that surrounded it, and she told them she'd leave the word the way it was. ***It's a Little Known Fact*** that Kathryn Lee "Katie" Bates refused to toss her poem or take the word "beautiful" out of it. The poem is the one known today as "America the Beautiful."

Army Nurse

Clarisse Harlow had done and seen a lot of things in her life, but nothing had prepared her for this. This was just a little more than she expected. Oh, she thought the job would be tough and fraught with dangers, but this was much more. Clarisse was a field nurse with the Union Army during the Civil War. She was in places like Fredericksburg and Antietam. The wounded were everywhere, and sometimes it seemed that she couldn't get away from it no matter how far from the front she was. But when she was at the front, which she was frequently, it was war! It was at Fredericksburg, with the battle in full rage less than half a mile away, that she stepped outside the medical tent for a breath of fresh air. She had just been tending to a soldier who had lost a leg, and she dearly needed a moment of peace and to escape the smell of the blood for just a minute. She noticed a large group of civilians on the other side of a fence just a few yards away. She was shocked to see civilians so close to the battle lines. The people started shouting at her, and she went a little closer. Clarisse realized they were shouting out names, the names of their husbands and sons and brothers, wanting to know where they were, whether they were alive or dead. She told them that she didn't have any of that information. But she would never forget the look in the eyes of those relatives, wondering if they still had a brother or husband or father. The pain of those people from not knowing was an image was so powerful that it kept her awake night after night, and it stayed with her long after the war was over. One day, she heard that there were thousands of soldiers still unaccounted for. So she decided to do something about it. Clarisse went to the old Confederate prison camp at Andersonville, Georgia, where more than thirteen thousand Union prisoners had been held. Many of them had died there, and lay in unmarked graves. She made a list of the missing, and set about trying to get a list of the prisoners who'd been there. She compared the two, and within a few months, she was able to tell literally thousands of families where their loved ones were buried. Word got around about what Clarisse had done and people all over the country sent her letters with the names of their family members. She published her lists in the newspapers. She made flyers to put up in post offices everywhere, from Maine to Texas. She worked almost non-stop for three years at finding the soldiers. The U.S. government was so impressed that they established an Office of Missing Soldiers headed by Clarisse Harlow. She became the first woman to ever lead a government agency. By the time she was finished, Clarisse had located more than twenty-two thousand missing soldiers. Why have most Americans never heard about this woman who did so much good? Many have, because she went on to do even more. *It's a Little Known Fact* that the woman who was the first missing persons locator and was the first woman to lead a government agency, was the same woman who founded the American Red Cross... Clara Harlow Barton.

Chaz Allen

The Letters

He got the first one in 1775. It was a simple letter evidently written by someone who knew what was going on, and there was a lot going on. John Adams was in the middle of a coming revolution. He was talking daily to the influential people of the colonies about what was coming and how best to handle it. John Adams started receiving the letters and kept receiving them through the entire ordeal and into the White House. Adams was a lawyer and a man of letters and documents. He received quite a large amount of correspondence considering the times and the unreliable mail system back then. Much of it was people wanting him to represent them in a legal matter. But a growing amount was from people who knew of his affiliation with the leaders of the coming revolution. People were always writing to him and offering advice on what to do. Much of it was an appeal to break away from King George and the unfair practices of the ruling class. But, believe it or not, an almost equal amount came from people advising him to be quiet and let things be. Nearly half of the colonist in 1775 didn't want to break from England and the King. They liked the system that was in place and thought that independence would be the downfall of the colonies. But there was one person who seem to offer advice that was very well reasoned. The letters starting coming in 1775 when John was in the midst of drafting the Declaration of Independence along with Ben Franklin and Thomas Jefferson. The letter spoke eloquently about the need to abolish slavery and make all men free, black and white. Well, that didn't make it in the document, but John certainly knew how this person felt. More letters followed with more advice. Each letter was unsigned. But the writing was the same and they made references to previous letters, so Adams knew they were from the same person. John Adams became the second President and even in the White House, the letters continued to come, each with more advice about what yet needed to be done. Adams confided to his aid that perhaps, more than anyone else, the writer of these letters spoke the truth about what needed to be done to build the country. If he could only find out who was writing them, he would invite him to the White House and thank him for the years of advice and counsel that had guided him all those years. Well, he never did find out who it was, but we know today. We know because the writer had an accomplis, someone to mail the letters when they couldn't. ***It's a Little Known Fact*** that the secret writer of the letters that so influenced John Adams in the creating of the Declaration of Independence and as President, was in fact his own wife Abigail Adams.

Connie's Mentor

Most young people have someone that they look up to, sometimes an adult, but usually someone closer to their own age. Young people can't always identify with an adult for things like clothes or music, but someone a year or two older? Now that's a different story. An older bother or sister maybe, perhaps someone at school a grade or two ahead. That's how it was for Connie. She was a student at Montgomery Blair High School. So was Jean, the young woman who Connie admired. She was a year ahead of Connie and was a teacher's assistant in her chemistry class. Jean was a tall slender girl who always sat straight. "She had unbelievable posture" said Connie, "and a pair of legs that every girl in school would have given anything to have." Yes, Jean was a pretty girl and quite intelligent as well. Most of the kids at Montgomery Blair thought so, and she was admired. Jean was not only smart, but she also had a flair for the dramatic. She said she got that from her mother. Jean's mom was a Jewish jewelry wholesaler. Her dad was a good man from Arkansas who dabbled in several businesses. Jean was popular, a good conversationist, and she seemed to have a real knack for helping younger kids. So was it any wonder that Connie found Jean to be a good role model? Jean was also a great dancer. She had been taking dance lessons most of her life and was always in a school play or some kind of talent contest. Jean was going to be a dancer when she grew up, and that's where she and Connie saw things differently. Connie didn't have any intention of becoming a dancer. She had her eye on the broadcasting business. And even though the two young women had different goals in life, Connie still found Jean to be an inspiration. It must have worked, because Connie did do well in life. Most people know Connie quite well. Her face is on the television screen almost everyday and has been for years now. She one of the best known television anchors in the business, and she is married to a famous broadcaster. Everyone has a mentor, and Jean was hers. ***It's a Little Known Fact*** that a young Connie Chung choose another successful woman to be her role model, although she couldn't have know at the time just how successful she would be. But she remembers that unbelievable posture and the spectacular legs of the teacher's assistant at the front of the class: Goldie Jean Hawn!

Pig Foot Mary

Arnold Dean was in a hurry. Arnold was a banker at famed First City Bank in New York and he was in charge of one of the biggest accounts at the bank: that of Lillian Dean. Ms. Dean was one of the bank's largest depositors and he had just been summoned to her death bed. To say he was nervous was an understatement. What was she going to instruct him to do with all that money if she dies, he wondered. He had heard that she was sick, but he didn't realize it was so serious until the note came to the bank instructing him to come and bring documents to her house. She was too sick to come to the bank as she had for years. The frail old woman was known throughout both the bank and the financial district as being one of the shrewdest investors on Wall Street. In 1901, there weren't many woman investors at all. Lillian often came to the bank and told Arnold to invest money in this company or that deal that she had heard about. And almost without exception the tip was a good one and her fortune grew, and grew and grew. Other than being a financial genius, Lillian seemed perfectly normal, well with one exception: those pig feet. Everyday on the way to and from the bank, she stopped at a sidewalk vendor who was known as Pig Foot Mary's. It was a poor black woman who sold grilled pig feet, chitlings and corn on the cob from her street cart. That stuff will kill Lillian someday, Arnold used to say, and it looked like it finally had as he hurried to her home. When he arrived he was surprised to see that Lillian Dean's home was quite modest. It certainly wasn't representative of the fortune she had in his bank. But that wasn't the only surprise he got that day. No indeed! Lillian told Arnold a great secret. The secret was that she was not Lillian Dean at all. Her real name was Carrie Norman, but she had been acting as Lillian for years because the real Lillian Dean didn't think she would be welcome in his bank. Well, after he recovered, Arnold said that if she told him the real identity of the millionaire, he would see to it that all was taken care of properly. Arnold couldn't have been more surprised when she told him. ***It's a Little Known Fact*** that one of the richest depositors and most savoy investors in the early 1900's was standing in front of the bank the whole time...at a vendor cart. Yes, Lillian Dean was Pig Foot Mary. She had spent years listening to bankers and investors and everyone on the street talking openly in front of her about the most secret of business deals, never suspecting that Mary was listening. She decided that she would take a little of the advice for herself. She amassed a fortune of over a million dollars and because of her friend Carrie's honesty, Pig Foot Mary was able to enjoy it for the rest of her life.

Bullet Proof

The young policeman was nervous, and he had good reason to be. The angry armed robber was holding an elderly lady in front of him as he moved out of the bank to his waiting car. Slowly and carefully, the young policeman stood up from his position behind his patrol car and moved toward the desperate man and the terrified lady. It was a brave thing to do but he knew he must. Suddenly, the nervous young robber pushed the lady aside and ran for the car, taking a shot at the approaching policeman. The shot was accurate and the bullet caught the brave young officer in the middle of his chest. He felt the strong thump from the bullet and then dove to cover the old woman, now crouching on the ground. In one sure swift motion, he took a shot at the fleeing robber and his aim was perfect. He caught him in the back of the leg, just enough to bring him down, giving enough time for the other policemen on the scene to rush in and kick the gun from his hand and throw him to the ground, ending the what could have been a deadly episode. The nerve-racking scene was just one of hundreds that are played out every day as the police try to keep the public safe from the bad guys. And the brave men in uniform are able to make that courageous move because, well, because S.L. Kwolek did not have enough money for medical school. Kwolek was born in Pennsylvania in 1923 and knew tough times right from the beginning. The senior Kwolek died just a few years later and his wife was left to raise two children by herself, just as the Great Depression was beginning. Despite the tough times, Mrs. Kwolek made sure that her children received an education. Why, S.L. Kwolek even managed to get a degree from college in 1946 and was hoping to go to medical school. But there was no money. However, there was a job at the Dupont Company in Buffalo, New York. There the young graduate not only went to work but went on to excel in the company. Among the many inventions credited to S.L. Kwolek is an amazing fiber that is five times stronger than steel. This versatile fiber, called kevlar, is used in radial tires, racing sails, fiberoptic cable, spacecraft shells, bridge suspension cables, and kevlar is also the material inside a policeman's bullet proof vest. ***It's a Little Known Fact*** that because Stephanie Louise Kwolek did not have enough money for medical school, she went on to become one of top women inventor's of the twentieth century.

A Strange Canvas

Funny as it may seem, we don't know her first name—only that she was the daughter of a shopkeeper named Rufas Skeel. But we do know that she had an eye for beauty, and she was quite an artist. She loved to painted still lifes, and that took up most of her spare time. Miss Skeel didn't sit around painting all day, though. She had to attend to her chores of sewing and needlework, as was expected of all young ladies in the 1800's. But one day while browsing around in her father's store, she found some really fine muslin fabric from a textile mill owned by Benjamin and Robert Knight. She loved the new fabric. The soft texture felt good on your skin and it was easy to cut and sew. But the customers seemed to be ignoring it. Well, she knew that if the customers just tried it, they would like this wonderful muslin, but she didn't quite know how to make the plain white cloth seem more attractive. She worried it around in her head for a while and finally came up with a grand idea. Miss Skeel went to work with her paints and paper and made several paintings of a swar apple, a family favorite at the Skeel house. When the paintings of the rosey apples were dry, she pasted them to the muslin material—and sure enough, the cloth with the painting attached was the first to sell. In fact, the paintings were so popular that soon she was painting grapes, pears and cherries to paste onto the Knight Mills material, too. Now, this was quite a departure from the normal. Material up to that point was kind of like a Model T: you could have any color you wanted, as long as it was black. Well, not all fabric was black of course, but designs on fabric was nearly unheard of. A few pin stripes here and there, and that was about it! So when this young woman started decorating some of the fabric, people really took notice. Robert Knight, the owner of the textile mill, took notice pretty quick that one store was selling more of his new cloth than nearly all the others combined. The little country store was selling quite of few of the mill's materials. Robert knight decided to investigated personally and found that Miss Skeel's artwork was making the difference, and that gave him an idea. He talked it over with his brother and soon the young woman's pictures were copied and printed and appeared as labels on all the cloth that came from the Knights' mill. That was in 1871. Before long, the labels showed a combination of an apple, some grapes and some gooseberries, and still do today. It's a Little Known Fact that one young lady's love of painting and wonderful imagination led to the first label ever used on a bolt of cloth, and to what we know today as 'Fruit of the Loom.'

The Scene

It just wasn't going right, and it was so important that this did go just right. Vina was trying, but it just wasn't coming out the way it should. The director came over and asked Vina what the problem was. After all, she was a seasoned actress and had done dozens of scenes before a camera. Vina said she wasn't sure, but she was. She was suppose to lie on the special prop that had been built for the scene and scream. She knew how to scream, but when the time came she just couldn't. She would lay back and start crying. The director and the crew were baffled. Why was she crying? Well, the reason was very personal. It all started for Vina when she was just 4 years old in Canada. One very cold and blustery day in the midst of the Canadian winter, Vina was being pulled across a lake on her sled by her eleven-year-old brother and his friend. The trio was about halfway across the lake when they hit a crack in the ice. Suddenly Vina's

49

brother was in the water over his head and Vina and the sled were sliding in right behind him. The water was freezing cold and Vina didn't know how to swim. Her brave young brother seemed to sense what to do, though. He righted himself and lifted Vina out of the water. Vina struggled to get back on the ice and solid footing, but she kept slipping back into the freezing lake. Finally her brother simply held her up out of the water in safety until his friend ran for help. Rescue came in time for Vina, but not her brother. He died saving his little sister. Now, 20 years later in the middle of this movie set, every time Vina laid her head back and got into the position that the scene required, she remembered that day and her brother and the tears flowed. *It's a Little Known Fact* that it took a very long time to get that scene right, but they did, and it became one of the biggest movies of its time. It is still revered today as a marvel of special effects and movie making. One young actress had to overcome her past and her memories to get it right, every time she...Vina

Fay Wray ... laid back on the giant hand of King Kong!

The House That Sarah Built

You might call it the house that Sarah built, mostly because Sarah built it! Not actually with her hands, but she was there for every single nail that was driven. And there were a lot of nails. San Jose, California, is the place Sarah choose to build her house. It was one of the most unusual houses ever seen, and certainly one of the biggest! The house covered six acres. It didn't just sit on six acres. All six acres were under roof. Sarah's house had a hundred and sixty rooms, ten thousand windows, four hundred and sixty seven doors, fifty two sky-lights, forty seven fireplaces, forty stairways, thirteen bathrooms and six kitchens. Each and every one of the ten thousand windows had thirteen panes, each wall had thirteen panels, each closet had thirteen hooks and each chandelier had thirteen globes. Sarah was just a little superstitious. But don't superstitious people usually to avoid the number thirteen? Most hotels do. But not

Sarah. It was the perfect number for her guests. Sarah was a wealthy woman. When she started building her house in 1884, she had twenty million dollars. That's a lot of money today, but back then, it made her one of the richest people in the world. Sarah came from New Haven, Connecticut, where she was something of a society belle. She had everything; a loving husband, a beautiful little girl, and a ton f money. Then, suddenly, Annie died at only five weeks old. Before she and her husband could have another, he too died. How could fate be so cruel to her, she wondered. She slipped into depression and despair. Her precious daughter and loving husband were gone! That's when she decided that her money was the problem. It was the money or at least the source of her money which caused the premature deaths of the ones she loved the most. True or not, she believed it. Which is why she moved to San Jose and started building that big house, a house she kept working on 24 hours a day, 3 shifts never stopping, never resting, even for Christmas. The work on the house must continue. And it did, day and night, twenty four hours a day, for thirty seven years, until Sarah herself passed. The house is still there, and today visitors can see it any time and even take a tour- and maybe see her guests, though no one else ever has. ***It's a Little Known Fact*** that Sarah never once had a guest in her home. She lived there all by herself. She had built the house for guests you couldn't see -the dead, those that had died from the source of her money. She was Sarah Winchester, and she had inherited the Winchester fortune, money that came from the selling of the rifle that killed more Indians and soldiers than any other gun in the West. Sarah had built her house for them.

Julie's Secret

When young Julie McWilliams tucked the papers into her coat pocket and started down the deserted road, she had to wonder just what she'd gotten herself into. She was in a strange country, Ceylon, which today is known as Sri Lanka. She was supposed to meet a man she'd never seen before and give him an envelope full of documents. Not even Julie knew the exact nature of the documents she was carrying. Above all, she could never speak to anyone about what she was doing. Julie had certainly come a long way from her home in California, where she'd been fairly undistinguished, except for the fact that she was the tallest girl in her high school graduating class. Julie was six-feet-two! She came from a well-to-do family and she'd gone to an exclusive prep school. She had no trouble getting into an impressive college. But, like so many other young people, Julie never really knew what she wanted to do with her life. Not long after she finished college, World War II broke out and of course everything changed That's what put the young Miss McWilliams on the strange road thousands of miles from home. She saw the man standing at the corner just as she'd been told he would be. She gave him the envelope. Neither of them said a word. The man walked away and left Julie standing there. Once again, she had accomplished her mission. The tall, gangly California girl had passed on documents vital to the Allied war effort in the Asian campaign. She was a secret courier for the Office of Strategic Services -the forerunner of today's CIA. Julie was one of America's foremost couriers both in Ceylon and China. She passed on some of the most highly sensitive intelligence information of the entire war. While in China, she met and fell in love with an American foreign service officer, and she married him shortly after the war was over. With her own service finished, she settled into life as a diplomat's wife, and she and her husband were posted to Paris. And that's where her life changed again. She began to learn about

French cooking, and she's devoted herself to it ever since. ***It's a Little Known Fact*** that the tall California girl who worked in her country's spy service became the best-known chef in the world: Julia Child.

The Canning Lady

There have been several advancements in the Armed Forces over the years: the speed and agility of the aircraft in the Air Force, the maneuverability of the Army Tanks, and the ships of the Navy have certainly seen some incredible advances. There are now nuclear powered submarines and ships that can stay at sea as long as they want. The atomic fuel can last for 500 years, so as long as supply ships pull up along side and bring fresh food, water, and sailors, the ships almost never have to dock. That's pretty spectacular. So is the advent of the submarine. But without one major advance which happened nearly 100 years ago, a submarine or any of the other advances wouldn't be possible. At one time all ships were powered by wind. That was the best power source they had at the time. That's fine for many pleasure and merchant ships, but a war ship can't depend on something as unpredictable as the wind, especially if the enemy has something better. That's why coal-burning ships were developed. But that required huge bins in the bottom of the ships that held mountains of coal and enormous furnaces to burn the coal, and huge water reserves to turn the water into steam and power the propellers. That did work, pretty well as a matter of fact, but it sure was a lot of trouble. It was heavy and bulky and could never get much power really. Remember that the Titanic was a coal burner. When oil was discovered, many people had the idea to use oil to power the war ships. That would work great: less weight, more room on the ship, and much more power. But there was a problem-a big problem! Unlike coal, oil is extremely volatile. It blows up if there is not a good fuel regulator to keep the fire away from the stored oil. And many ships didn't have one! Until the day when a canning expert was told by a spiritualist to go to the Pennsylvania oil field and invent a way to allow the oil rigs to burn off excess gas from the wells. The result was the Automatic Safety Burner. It was a real boon to the oil business, but it also attracted the attention of the

United States Navy. They saw the Automatic Safety Burner as a way to put oil power on Navy ships without them blowing up from their own fuel. That may well be the single most important advancement in ship development. And it was invented by a person who had already made a name for themselves and a small fortune in inventing a better canning method for food. *It's a Little Known Fact* that she did! Yes -she! Amanda Jones was the woman who invented the Automatic Safety Burner and put the power in the United States Navy.

The Nightmare

Have you ever had a bad dream? A nightmare? Most of us have. And although they're not too pleasant, we know that it was just a bad dream. We wake up and we're safe in our bed, in our own room, and it was just a dream after all. But that's not the way it is for some people. Some have recurring nightmares. The same dark foreboding images return again and again. Sometimes every night. That was the case with Lou. As a fairly young woman she fell ill. Her illness kept her bed ridden for quite a long while. It may have been a physical aliment, but it had a serious affect on her psychological state of mind. She began having nightmares, and she had them every night for years. It was the same reoccurring dream that tormented her night after terrifying night. Lou dreamed that she was being chased by a big Spanish man. Sometimes he was dressed as a conquistador, sometimes not. Sometimes he was on a horse, sometimes not. Some nights he would be laying in ambush for Lou, and other times he would simply come out of nowhere and chase her. The situation wasn't always the same, but it was always the same Spanish man. Almost every night he caught her and molested her. For whatever reason, in her own mind Lou never got away. Her tormenter always caught her and she would wake up screaming in terror. She could never get back to sleep again. Sleep became an enemy. She feared it as much as the dream itself. But Lou didn't know any Spanish men, conquistadors or otherwise. As far as she knew, she had never heard anything about such a man molesting any of her family, friends or anyone else. It seemed that this was a completely irrational dream. It's interesting that someone can have something bother them for years and not have any idea where all the horror and sleepless nights are coming from. Lou did finally recover from her illness, at least well enough to write a book. That's the first thing she did after she recovered. And what a book it was, probably read by more women than any other book in history.

Did the book have anything to do with the years of sleepless nights? ***It's a Little Known Fact*** that the woman who was so badly tormented by nightmares did go on to write one of the most popular books of all time, and "Lou" Louisa May Alcot called it "Little Women."

A Wise Brownie

Earl grew up in New Hampshire. He was quiet, reserved, but always thinking. Everyone said that he was a clever fellow who would probably do all right. Back in the thirties, the oil business was the biggest thing going, and Earl figured that there was a lot of money to be made in the by-products of the oil refining process. During World War II, Earl made a very big contribution to the safety of all the troops down in the trenches. This was a war when one of the biggest dangers was what we today call chemical warfare. The American soldiers didn't care what it was called as long as they had some way to protect themselves from the deadly gas. There were gas masks, all right, but they were still kind of primitive and didn't always work right. Earl figured out a way to take petroleum by-products and mold them into little tubes and hoses that kept the air flowing in the military gas mask. If that was all he had done, you probably wouldn't know his name. But you do. When the war ended, Earl kept tinkering with this new material he had discovered. It was strong and durable and could be made into many different shapes. Now, not every home in America needed a gas mask, but what was it that could be used in every kitchen in the country? That's where Earl's ingenuity came in. How did he figure it out? Well, he stood in the kitchen and watched until it hit him. Then he had it: the product America was waiting for. He had finally come up with the idea, but he couldn't seen to get anyone interested in it. That was when Earl got together with a woman named Brownie Wise, a friendly, out-going lady who invited several of her friends over to her house to show them what Earl had invented. And with that, an American institution was born. *It's a Little Known Fact* that the same material that was used to make gas masks during the war was eventually re-designed into something that made millions for Earl Tupper!

Chaz Allen

First Prisoners

Have you ever wondered who were the rowdiest rebels were during the American Revolution? Just take a look at Massachusetts. When Samuel Adams and the Sons of Liberty dressed up like Indians and dumped 343 chests full of tea into Boston Harbor, well, it was business as usual for these guys. But it did make the British a sight madder than they had been. They closed down the harbor and swore they'd stomp out the rebellion in a matter of days. The truth is, the British really weren't too worried about the Colonial uprising. They thought if they sent out a ship or two, the rebels would turn and run. Royal officers told their men that the Colonials were "raw, undisciplined, cowardly men" and that "the very sound of a cannon will carry them off." To the British, these "urban rowdies" were just a bunch of smugglers, some buckskin-wearing frontiersmen, and a few deadbeat Southern planters. Sam Adams, John Hancock and the other leaders of the Massachusetts rebellion were down-right criminals fit only to hang. It was probably the day after Paul Revere took his ride through the country side that the English first lost a bit of their cocky attitude. On April 19, 1775, the very day that the famous shot was heard around the world, British troops suffered their first defeat at the Battle of Concord. The American Revolutionaries were so mad that they chased the British all the way from Concord up through Lexington and straight back to Boston. But that wasn't the only lesson the British learned that day. If England had wanted to know how hard these rag-tag soldiers would be to defeat, all they had to do was look closely at the squabble at Menotomy, a small settlement about an hour's march from Lexington. It so happens that a convoy of British soldiers were on their way to join the main regiment and took a wrong turn somewhere, and they came up against 12 old men who had been left to defend that village. To the surprise of the British, these ancient warriors opened fire. The English soldiers who didn't fall in that first volley of muskets turned and ran through town, throwing their arms into a passing pond. They eventually ran into an old woman digging dandelions in her garden, and to her they surrendered. ***It's a Little Known Fact*** that the first prisoners of the American Revolution were the trophy of Mother Batherick, a grandmother many times over.

Indentured Servant

He could see what was happening from his hiding place in the trees. It was dangerous for him to be this close to the house, but that's the way General Sam Houston was. He had to see things for himself and make his own assessment. The man he was watching was none other than General Antonio Lopez de Santa Anna. The Mexican dictator had been staying at Morgan Plantation ever since he took it by force 5 five days ago. Of course that wasn't all that hard to do, since the owner, Colonel James Morgan was down around Galveston with his regiment, leaving his plantation unguarded. The only one there was Morgan's indentured servant Emily West. Emily was a slave, or as close to it as a white woman could get back then. The Colonel had bought her, paid cash, and she was bound to him for seven years. It was Emily that was keeping General Santa Anna at the Morgan plantation. Emily was a beautiful woman. The

Colonel wrote that she had hair the color of a red rose and skin of alabaster that seem to glow. We do have a picture of her and she was lovely indeed. Santa Anna was known for his weakness for pretty women to begin with, and now he delayed his march north against the Texicans just to spend some time with Emily. One of Santa Anna's Lieutenant's said that it was as if the General was mesmerized by her. That's where Sam Houston caught up with him. Emily played the gracious host, even though this man was the enemy, because she knew that if she could get the dictator to sit still, the Americans could mount an attack. And that is just what Sam Houston did. One morning when Santa Anna was pursuing Emily rather than taking care of business, Houston attacked. Even though the Americans were outnumbered by a two to one margin, they defeated Mexican Army and the Battle of San Jacinto was over in less than twenty minutes. One Mexican soldier said that the sight of Santa Anna running around during the attack in his underwear and red slippers just didn't give the men any courage. It was over. Houston was mighty grateful to Emily for what she did. So was most of Texas. They even wrote a song about Emily. ***It's a Little Known Fact*** that General Santa Anna and the Mexican Army were defeated by Sam Houston because he was distracted by the indentured servant woman of Colonel Morgan, the very beautiful Emily D. West, better known as the Yellow Rose of Texas!

She Was Boss

Edith was a widow at forty-three. She really hadn't given any thought to getting married again. Her late husband had been a wealthy jeweler and left her financially secure. Her days were spent in the company of good friends and a number of social functions. She had decided she didn't need another man in her life. Until fate played its hand. Edith had accepted an invitation to tea from a friend. The tea was being held at the home of her friend's cousin, who was a well-known and powerful man. As Edith and her friend were enjoying the socializing, the gentleman of the house arrived. Edith was almost instantly smitten with the man. And why not -he was well-spoken, mannerly, and cultured. He was fifteen years older than Edith, and he was a widower himself. One thing led to another, as things do, and Edith married Woody a few months later. She was absolutely devoted to him, and he to her. They traveled everywhere together, and he consulted her on all decisions, whether large or small. One of Woody's friends grumbled that it was impossible to talk to him anymore, because Woody was always busy whispering to Edith. It wasn't long before Edith wielded a little influence of her own, and she used it to support her husband's many projects. By all accounts, they were one of the happiest, most successful couples in America. But then Woody became very ill. Many said that he was never the same. Some of his closest associates suggested that he should step down from his position. Woody seemed to agree. Edith, on the other hand, would hear none of it! When the same "gentlemen" asked who was going to do his job, she said that she'd do it herself! And she did. She set it up so that the only people who were able to see Woody were herself and his doctor. She threw herself into his job. She signed off on all major projects, and started new ones. When some of the underlings grumbled about the way things were being run, she fired them and replaced them with people she knew were loyal to her husband. She was tough in negotiations with his rivals, and she never gave an inch. Edith made it clear that she spoke for her husband, and if someone didn't like it, she showed them the door. By all accounts, she ran things! And it appears she ran them as well as her husband did, maybe even better. Through all this, she protected her husband and his condition. She hadn't allowed any public announcements about his illness. As far as the rest of world was concerned, everything was normal. Never mind that he wasn't seen in public for nearly three years! Well, finally the time came for Edith and her husband to retire, and she took care of him until the day he died. She was a remarkable woman. ***It's a Little Known Fact*** that although the country has never elected a woman president, there was one, and a good one. Edith Wilson served in her husband's absence, almost completely running the country after her husband, Woodrow Wilson, suffered a stroke.

It Was Her Son

Mary didn't like all the turmoil that was going on in America. It seemed she didn't even recognize her home anymore. Social change was everywhere, and the whole fabric of society was falling to pieces. Violence was starting to break out. Even outside the city, far out in the countryside where Mary and her family lived, the changes could be seen. Young people no longer had respect for the government. They said the government was corrupt and immoral, and some were even refusing to recognize the government anymore. Mary was horrified when her own son started to say some of these things. He'd always been smart as a boy, though a bit headstrong, but Mary thought she'd raised him right so that he knew how to show the proper respect for authority. But he was a grown man now, and she couldn't control him. He started going to meetings and hanging around with people that Mary didn't approve of. They were putting strange ideas in her son's head, and he was going along with them! After a time, it seemed to Mary that her boy—the boy she'd raised so well—was in fact one of the leaders of this group of rebellious good-for-nothings! Well, that did it. She finally confronted her son and told him to stay away from those characters he'd been seeing, to stop all the foolish talk and to remember who he was and where he came from. For a long time, her son just stared at her. When he finally spoke, he tried to tell her what he believed, and that change was necessary, and it was coming, like it or not. He finally told her that he would use whatever means possible to help the changes along. Mary couldn't believe what she was hearing! Her own son, her flesh and blood, talking about tearing down all the institutions of government. She had raised him better than that. She wouldn't hear of it—she called her son a traitor and banished him from her house. It hurt her to do it to her own son, but Mary was a woman of principle and she wouldn't betray her principles, not even for her family. Mary lived another twenty years, but she never, ever forgave him for his treason. It may be hard to believe, but it's true, all of it! ***It's a Little Known Fact*** that the mother who became estranged from her son over his politics was Mary Washington, mother of George.

Hello Central

Erna was in the hospital when she got her idea. There wasn't anything wrong with her, she was just giving birth to one of her three daughters and she had time on her hands. At that time women would be in the hospital for up to two weeks after giving birth and there was lots of time to think. Erna Schneider Hoover was what some might call well-rounded. She studied medieval history at Wellesley, and unlike most of her friends she didn't get married right away, but went on to Yale where she earned her doctorate in philosophy and mathematics. After that, she did what was expected of her for a little while. She taught at Swarthmore college. But then she quit teaching altogether to go into research for Bell Laboratories, not the kind of thing a wife and mother was expected to do in 1954. But Erna wasn't your average sort of woman, so this move didn't really surprise anyone. And having a baby? Well, that was no different! So, Erna was in the hospital nursing her baby with plenty of time to think about things. For a philosophy and mathematics major, just having a baby opens up all sorts of speculations and questions. She was especially fascinated with the way the hospital handled certain tasks. Here was a facility full of people, all of whom were in need of very special care and attention. Erna watched carefully as the nurses use a systematic method of getting to all of the patients. She started drawing out a schematic of how nurses moved through their duties. That prompted her to think about a particular problem at Bell Labs. Before long, Erna was sketching out a solution. In the mid 1950's, Bell was having a terrible time handling all the telephone calls the phone system was expected to carry. The hardwired, mechanical switching systems were being overwhelmed. You may remember the women at the switchboard, pulling plugs and inserting plugs, and that's how phone systems worked back then. ***It's a Little Known Fact*** that Erna Schneider Hoover got the idea for a computerized switching system for telephone calls while she was in the hospital. She was also granted one of the first software patents ever issued. Next time you pick up a phone, remember the woman who made that possible…while having a baby!

Torpedo

During a war, patriotism is usually at an all-time high. And that's the way it was during World War II. Everyone wanted to be part of the war effort, even those whose day-to-day duties lay far from the front. At a fashionable dinner party one night in 1940, a popular composer named George Antheil was doing his part by performing for a benefit. That night his inspiration had come from a beautiful young Viennese woman his hostess had seated right next to him. She was lovely! She was without a doubt one of the most beautiful women George Antheil had even seen, and he wasn't the only one who thought so. The young woman was attracting the attention of nearly everyone at the party. Even though Ms. Markey was new to America, she shared in America's patriotic sentiments. She had even been thinking about a military innovation which she thought might help the Allies win the war. She shared her thoughts with the musician. Antheil listened intently as she described her idea: a device that would send radio commands to torpedoes in coded patterns, enabling the weapon to be guided without being jammed by enemy. The idea was a good one and there was something about it Antheil knew rang a bell with him. But he just couldn't put his finger on it. Suddenly the answer came to him. Player pianos! Of course! The beautiful young Ms. Markey had been describing the design for a variable radio tuner whose frequency was changed from time to time by punched instructions in a belt. The design was almost identical to that of a player piano. The two might actually be on to something? That evening was the beginning of an intense collaboration between a radiantly beautiful Viennese inventor and an American composer. The team stayed together for two years working out problems with the design and rethinking their project. Finally in 1942 they were ready. They applied for and received a patent. Antheil sometimes wondered if his partner's inspiration came from her past. She had, after all, been briefly married to Friedrich Mandl, one of the world's leading munitions tycoons. That was, of course, before she came to the States to start her new career. And she did pretty well with that, too. She was called by some the world's most beautiful woman, and Hollywood's most glamorous star. **It's a Little Known Fact** that the woman who invented the radio coding device that so significantly helped the Allies win the war was the lovely and elegant film star Hedy Lamarr.

Staircase of Loretto

This true story centers around a little tiny chapel in Santa Fe, New Mexico. That's where the event took place, but that's not really the story. The chapel was built in 1610 by Mexican carpenters for the Sisters of Loretto. It was to be fashioned after the Saint-Chapelle in Paris, small with a choir loft in the rear. That's exactly what was done. But the builder got a few measurements wrong and the choir loft was inaccessible from the ground floor, except by ladder which the workmen used. Since this was the first time the local workmen had ever seen such a chapel, much less built one, they didn't realize the error until the whole thing was finished. The sisters could not traverse the ladder, especially in the traditional clothing of their order. Carpenter after carpenter was consulted, and they all said the same thing: a staircase built now would extend completely into the middle of the chapel. They would lose most of the capacity. It appeared that nothing could be done. But the sisters prayed about it, constantly for nine days! And it was on the ninth and last day that a gray-haired man leading a donkey and carrying a tool chest stopped at the convent. He said that he had heard of the sister's problem and had a solution. He really didn't look like he had much of anything, but the sister's had a choir loft they couldn't ever get to, so he was welcome to try. And he did. He worked quietly and alone, with no other help at all. For eight months the carpenter labored, using the crudest set of hand tools. Then suddenly, it was finished. The sister's knew because the carpenter was gone. No goodbye, no payment asked for or given. Nothing! He was gone in the middle of the night! The staircase looked like no other the nuns had ever seen. It was a narrow graceful spiral of thirty-three steps that completed two three-hundred and sixty-degree turns between the ground and the loft. And there was no center support! Each piece of precession fit to every other. No banister, no support. It looked like it would fall the first moment anyone stepped foot on it. But it didn't, and it hasn't! Even now, one hundred and forty years later, it still stands and is used daily. It's still there and visitors are welcome. The Sister's of Loretto will say that the gray-haired man was the answer to their prayers. But there is one more thing that is strange about this story, and it's also true. ***It's a Little Known Fact*** that the wood the carpenter used to build the now famous staircase is not local to the region. As a matter of fact, it can't be found anywhere in New Mexico or Arizona. And even though a very through search has been done, no record exists anywhere of any lumber supplier selling such wood to anyone, much less a carpenter leading a donkey.

*Extraordinary Women -The Things
They Have Done, That You Never Knew*

Spinning Wheel

Most of the really big inventions happen by accident and one never know who's going to come up with one next. That was the case with Sister Tabitha. She was a quiet woman of devout religious convictions. Actually she was a Shaker. Not many are left anymore, but at one time there were quite a few in this country. They were called Shakers because when they prayed and got into the spirit, they would shake when the spirit of God came upon them. That made some folks laugh and scared others. But they were an ingenious group of people. Believe it or not, many of the modern conveniences that are enjoyed today are owed to the Shakers who lived a couple of hundred years ago. What conveniences? Well, the washing machine! The Shakers made the first washing machines. They also invented the clothes pin and a cotton fabric that didn't need ironing. Now, Sister Tabitha wasn't a nun. But most of the women of this religious order were called sister. Tabitha loved to work at her spinning wheel. It was said that she was fast as lightening on her spinning wheel. She would spin yarn for her family and several of the other families, mostly because she was so good at it. Her yarn was known to be tight and firm, good for knitting and making clothes. One day she was watching her husband work at building a new addition to their barn. It was a real chore to build that structure. Because there were no mills in the area, every piece of wood had to be cut from a tree, hand sawed and planed smooth before it could then be cut it to size and put it up on the barn. That's a lot of work just to get one board up. But that's the way it was. Sister Tabitha was sitting at the window one day watching this process while spinning yarn. The more she looked the clearer it became, and it didn't take long for her to act. She got up and without saying a word to her husband, she headed for the tool shed. What happened next changed the way men have built homes, barns and buildings for the next two hundred years. ***It's a Little***

Known Fact that from watching the action of her spinning wheel, Sister Tabitha, a Shaker woman, invented a tool that has saved millions of labor intensive hours. Yes, mostly men use it, but a women invented it: the buzz saw!

Tyrannical Husband

Calvin was a tyrant! Just about as mean spirited and demeaning as a man can get. He was ill tempered, fussy and hard to get along with. Especially to his wife, but she put up with it. Calvin would order his wife and family around and keep them hopping day and night. If they didn't follow his orders, they'd get a beating. He would demand that dinner was made and on the table at a certain time, whether he was home or not. And if he was late, it better still be warm. He had to have the furniture in the house arranged a certain way. No one was permitted to make a sound when he was reading or relaxing, or just trying to get his thoughts as he would call it. His wife once said that she wasn't sure he had any thoughts. Except his impulses, that is. Calvin would frequently come up with a hair brained scheme and go off on a tangent. He would upset the whole family and cause everyone a ton of useless work. And most of that fell to his wife. He literally treated her like a slave. He did nothing and insisted that she wait on him hand and foot. To make matters worse, about a year into the marriage, he became ill with indigo and was bedridden. He turned into a monster when he was sick. That must have been quite hard for his wife, because she came from a solid family with a good, gentle and loving father. In her father's home, there was safety, security and love. She had expected that it would be the same in her husband's home. But it was a rude awakening. Calvin would beat her and even make her sleep on the floor on the coldest nights rather than let her into his bed and possibly disrupt his sleep. She worked like a slave without thanks, recognition or gratitude. It was, by her own admission, a horrible existence. Her story is known today because she wrote about it, and so much more. ***It's a Little Known Fact*** that the woman who was treated like a slave in her own home later wrote a book that would tell everyone the plight of all oppressed people. Much of "Uncle Tom's Cabin" was really about author Harriet Beecher Stowe's own life.

Because of Mom

Harry Burn scrambled through an office window in the Tennessee State Capitol building and crept along a third floor ledge to escape the angry mob that was chasing him. He inched his way along the ledge and managed to get into the attic, where he hid until his pursers gave up the hunt. The people chasing Harry were all wearing red roses on their jacket lapels, and just a few minutes earlier had been his friends and allies. What could cause such a change? Well, it was August and the weather was hot. The Tennessee State Capitol building was like a sauna inside. That seemed to fuel the short tempers of the legislators who had come together in a special session to debate the Constitutional amendment before them. Debate is a nice word for what was going on. For days and days they argued, fought, yelled and tried to influence the other side. But they were still deadlocked. At twenty-four-years-old Harry Burn was the youngest representative in State Legislature, and as it happened, his vote was crucial. Representatives had to make a decision that would change history. Not only for Tennessee, but also the history of the United States. Thirty-five states had already ratified the amendment they were debating, and one more would make it law. The amendment would be added to the Constitution of the United States. Those against ratification all wore red roses on their lapels. The pro-ratification side wore yellow roses. Harry Burn wore a red rose. So why was he hiding in the attic of the Capitol with his own red rose-wearing allies out to get his blood? We'll get to that. All of a sudden the red rose-wearing Speaker of the House moved to table the amendment, which would have buried it. But the table vote was a tie and the Speaker had no choice but to call the measure to a ratification vote. One by one, the members called out their choices. Aye. Nay. They all sweltered in the stifling heat and worried. The vote was going to be close. In the midst of all this, a messenger arrived with a telegram for Harry. The telegram had a yellow rose attached to it. It was from Harry's mother back in Niota, Tennessee. She had been reading about the speeches in the newspapers and was offering some advice. Harry agonized over the decision before him. His resolve was wavering. What would he do? His colleagues expected his support, but his mother had always given him good advice. Then it was time to vote. When they called Harry's name he voiced a resounding "Aye!" Upon hearing this unexpected change in Harry's vote, the Speaker also changed his vote and the amendment was ratified by the slimest of margins. Just what could make a young man take his life in his hands to cast such an unpopular vote? Harry said later, 'I know that a mother's advice is always best for her boy to follow, and my mother wanted me to vote for ratification." ***It's a Little Known Fact*** that in 1920 a mother from a tiny town in Tennessee was the deciding factor in influencing her son Harry to change his vote, and thereby ratify a Constitutional amendment giving women the right to vote. A mother's advice is never wasted!

The Publisher

Remember Sarah Hale? Most people do, though they don't know why. She was born in 1788, the same year that the Constitution was written. She grew up in a country where there weren't too many rules. She was a farmer's daughter from New Hampshire and Sarah did what all of her friends were doing. She grew up and married and started having babies. That is until her husband suddenly died. She found herself at 34 years old, with 5 children, no husband, no income, no job, and no skills. It would be a pretty tough spot for anyone. But Sarah soon proved that she was made of the same metal that founded this country. She did the only thing she knew how: she wrote. Sarah noticed that no one was writing anything for women. Everything printed in the last few years had been about politics. So, she launched a publication called, "Ladies Magazine." It was a hit. Yes, it had some politics in it, but it had other things, like fashion, romance and an advice column. Ladies Magazine became so popular that it was considered the Bible for fashion and manners. Sarah was Heloise, Miss Manners, Betty Crocker and Dear Abby all rolled up into one. Now that she was the head of a successful business, she didn't forget the hard times after the death of her husband. She launched the Seamans' Aid Society to assist widows and orphans of lost sailors. It became the blue print for many more organizations, like the Police Aid, Army Aid and Fireman's Aid societies. Sarah is also the person who went on a crusade to make Thanksgiving an official holiday. She not only encouraged it in her magazine and got the women of America behind it, but she went to Capitol Hill and made a personal appeal to Congress. And of course it worked. And with all this, her name still may not sound familiar. But she did one other thing, something she wrote as a small political commentary on good manners and polite society. Many think it is just a children's rhyme, but it wasn't. ***It's a Little Known Fact*** that the woman who was responsible for the first woman's magazine, the Seaman's Aid Society and getting Thanksgiving officially sanctioned as an American holiday, wrote one of the most famous poems of all time: Mary Had a Little Lamb!

A Farmers Wife

Anna was born in the mountains of upstate New York in 1860. She was one of ten children born to farmer Russell Robertson and his wife Margaret. The Robertsons were poor. Formal education was considered a luxury, so Anna left home at the age of 12 and went to work for other families—cooking, cleaning, ironing, gardening and taking care of the sick. At 17, she married Tom Man, who like her father was a hired man on a farm. And like her mother, she bore her husband ten children, though only five of them survived. It would be nice to think that life got easier for Anna after she married Tom, but it didn't. It seemed that a life of backbreaking work was Anna's destiny. Even her honeymoon trip to North Carolina was a trip she and her husband took because they were supposed to begin work there as caretakers of a horse ranch. But that fell through, so Anna and Tom found work on a dairy farm instead. In addition to bearing and taking care of children and a home, Anna did farm chores, including hand churning as much as 160 pounds of butter a week. She was creative in finding ways to help put food on the table. Along with canning and baking, she took up needlework. When her husband Tom passed away after 40 years of marriage, she took over running the farm, too. After all, somebody needed to do it, and it's not as if hard work was anything new to Anna. One might think that Anna had an unhappy life. But Anna felt true joy in living and she shared it wherever she went. She also had a deep appreciation of beauty, and when she got too old to run the farm she took up needlework. But she didn't slack off on her cooking and canning. Her canned fruits and jam often brought prizes from the judges at the local fair. Anna worked at her needlecraft until her arthritis got so bad she had to quit. This was a hard pill to swallow for one so accustomed to hard work. Anna just wasn't the rocking chair type. So at the age of 78, she picked up a paintbrush and decided to put some of that beauty that she had been seeing and feeling her whole life on canvas. It's a Little Known Fact that had it not been for her arthritis, Anna Robertson Moses might never have picked up a paint brush, and Grandma Moses would have died without painting a single stroke.

Harry's Secret

Many have heard of it, but who knows how intense it really was? What is it? The Battle of Bull Run. One really could be talking about any battle of any war really. They're all bad. No good comes from all the killing and maiming of human life. Frontline battles are some of the most traumatic times anyone could face. And they often bring out the best and worst in a person. If you live, you'll know what you're made of. That was certainly the case for Harry T Burford. Most would say that Harry was made of the right stuff. Harry had been in a number of battles during the war, and the Battle of Bull Run was yet one more in which he was to face his fears and draw on his inner strengths to get him through. Those inner strengths had served him well over the past few years. In battle after battle, in hand to hand combat, and even charging in the face of enemy fire, Harry had more than held his own. In fact, Harry was considered one of the best and bravest soliders in the division. But Harry didn't have to be there. He wasn't a conscript, he wasn't drafted or forced to serve. He had volunteered and he could leave anytime he wanted to. Harry knew something that no one else knew, and if he was to tell the Army would send him home in a second. But he kept his mouth shut and served honorably in his division, commanded by Stonewall Jackson himself. And like all the officers and men in the division, Jackson had seen for himself the courage, bravery and determination of Harry Burford. Stonewall both praised and decorated Harry on four separate occasions for his bravery and leadership in battle. Harry was a hero and leader of men. But what Jackson didn't know, what no one knew, was that Harry hid every night. Not from fear of battle, but from discovery. Harry didn't have to be there. He volunteered for duty after a loved one was killed in the war. It was Harry's husband. ***It's a Little Known Fact*** that Harry Burford, four time decorated battlefield hero, was in reality Loreta Jauneta Velasquez …a woman.

The House in Greenwich

72 Bank Street! There wasn't all that much unusual about the house -red brick, fairly big, and roomy. What was unusual was who owned it and who lived there. At one time or another, almost every starving writer and actor in New York lived in this house. There wasn't a person aspiring to a Broadway career who didn't know about 72 Bank Street or it's owner Miss Marion. For years Greenwich Village has been the meeting place of the arts community in New York. The great and near great have called this section of the city home. Some of the best museums, cafes and small theaters are still located there. Not just actors and writers, but also composers, singers and great artists have called the Greenwich section of the Big Apple home at one time or another. And there was one house that almost every one of the them knew, or at least knew their way to. It was the red brick house. Marion was known as one of the biggest supporters of

105

young and starving actors and writers in town. She often fed them when they were hungry. She gave them a place to sleep and sometimes live until they could get established. She was always entertaining and her guest list would quite often read like a who's who of the art community. It was not only a privilege but an honor to be invited to one of Marion's grand parties. She made certain that her young and hungry artsy friends were at the head of the list. And maybe that's what the real attraction was: the rich and powerful of New York coming down to the Village, and mixing with the people on the cutting edge. And show up they did. Marion was a saint to the starving artist. Especially one young writer named Evertt Tanner III, who was Marion's nephew. He lived there with the starving actors and writers, and he too took to writing. He wrote of his experiences, of what happened in his house. The world took notice. ***It's a Little Known Fact*** that Evertt Tanner III used the pen name Patrick Dennis. Patrick Dennis was writing about his own aunt when he wrote the story that would be come a multi-million best seller, a Broadway musical hit, and a smash movie: his aunt Marion…Auntie Mame.

The Violin Maker

Virginia had a great passion in life, and that passion was for classical music. She had a day job, all right, and was pretty good at it, but nothing came close to her musical passion. She became quite accomplished on both the cello and the viola, but it wasn't enough for her to play the instruments. After a while, Virginia decided to try her hand at making the instruments. To everyone's surprise, even her own, she did very well. Her reputation spread, and even the famous violinist Isaac Stern purchased and frequently played a violin Virginia had made. Virginia was an absolute perfectionist. Everything about her instruments had to be just right or she'd scrap the whole thing and start over. The construction had to be perfect, the strings just so, right down to the kind of wood. She'd search all over for the right wood. She started one viola, finished the front part of the frame, but she wasn't satisfied with the wood for the back. So she started looking around—and looking and looking. Where did she finally find a piece of wood she thought was perfect? Well, it was a shelf inside a phone booth in New York City! This was at a time when phone booths still had nice shelves to hold the phone books. So Virginia called the phone company and asked if she could buy the shelf out of the booth. They thought she was crazy, of course, and told her no. She made outrageous offers of money for that little piece of wood, but the phone company wouldn't budge. Well, she had to have that piece of wood, so one night Virginia and a friend came up with a plan to steal the shelf out of the phone booth. She got it out, all right, but being a good citizen, she'd replaced it with another piece of wood. But then she ran into problems: the new piece wasn't the right size! It didn't fit the phone booth. Virginia and her friend became a little frantic, for they knew they had to replace that shelf. There was a hospital across the street from the booth, and they took the wood there to a restroom where Virginia's friend took a saw and started to fix the new shelf. Virginia stood guard, and when a nurse stopped and asked her what all the racket was in the restroom in the middle of the night, Virginia mumbled something about it being the only time workmen could get in there! Well, they finally replaced the shelf, the phone company never knew what happened, and Virginia finished her viola. By all accounts, it was one of the finest instruments she'd ever made. Virginia's name isn't remembered today for being a great musician or instrument maker, even though she was both. But her name does live on. People with children have heard Virginia's name mentioned in the delivery room right. That's right! Virginia was a doctor. ***It's a Little Known Fact*** that the wonderful musician and physician created a system for evaluating newborn babies to see if they needed special medical attention. It's probably saved the lives of millions of babies. It bears her name—the Apgar Score, created by Dr. Virginia Apgar.

For The Love of A Woman

Buck was a smart young man, so smart that he graduated from college before the age of twenty. He was determined to make a name for himself as a lawyer. He did it, too. Before he was thirty years old, he'd served a couple of terms in his state legislature. But it was through his law practice that he earned a fortune. A quarter of a million dollars was an incredible amount of money in the early 1800's. It was about that time that Buck fell in love for the first time with a beautiful young woman named Ann Coleman. As it happened, Ann was the heiress to one of the wealthiest families in America at the time. Her father had made a huge fortune himself in the Pennsylvania iron trade. Buck and his Ann were head over heels for each other, but there was a problem, an age-old problem for young couples. Ann's family didn't think Buck was good enough for her. They thought he was just after her money. Never mind all the money he'd

111

made in his law practice and the fact that he'd been a respected state legislator. Buck loved Ann deeply, but they couldn't get past her family. To make matters worse, a few local busybodies told Ann that Buck was keeping company with other women. It wasn't true, but Ann was so upset she sent Buck a letter breaking off the engagement, then refused to see him when he wanted to talk to her. She was too hurt. Sadly, Buck was innocent. It was all caused by wayward gossip. Before Buck could get through all the obstacles and explain to Ann, she died. In just four days, Ann Coleman was dead. It was never clear exactly what happened, but the general consensus seemed to be that she'd committed suicide by taking some kind of poison. The Coleman family blamed Buck and they wouldn't even let him attend the funeral. Poor Buck was full of grief for he woman he loved, and he couldn't even say a final goodbye. The rumors became so bad that the people in his hometown turned against him. Some said he may as well have given Ann the poison himself. None of it was true! Buck was shaken up pretty badly, and he told his family and the few friends who stood by him that he would never love again. His friends figured that was the grief talking, and that after a while he'd get over it and find another woman to make him forget all about Ann. But that didn't happen. Evidently, Buck was a one woman man, even though he never married that woman. He was never serious about another woman for the rest of his life. He threw himself into his work, becoming one of the most respected lawyers in America. He became interested in politics again and served under two different Presidents as an ambassador to Russia, then to England. His political fortunes got better and brighter as the years went by, even as the man himself grew more lonely and depressed. The country was going through hard times, and there was talk of a civil war. Buck was right in the middle of it, and many people blamed him when war did break out in 1861. It seems he couldn't win, no matter what he did. "Old Buck," as he was later known, lived to be seventy-seven, and when he died, he had a picture of Ann

Caroline Coleman clutched in his hand, nearly fifty years after her death. *It's a **Little Known Fact*** that our only bachelor President, James "Buck" Buchanan, spent his entire lifetime grieving over the loss of his one true love.

The Timid Lawyer

It's the kind of story that sit-coms are made out of, but this one really happened. It's just as well that it did, or she may never have started at all. Who? Well Elizabeth Hanford that's who. The young Ms. Hanford had already accomplish quite a bit in her life. She was young and in 1960 not too many women were moving into the ranks of professionals, much less something as demanding as law, but that was her dream. She approached it very seriously, graduating from one of the most prestigious law schools in the country: Harvard. She was only one of 24 women to do so that year out of 550 men. After law school, she didn't feel ready to start practicing law, so she got a job at the Department of Health in Washington DC. She would spend most of her off hours visiting courtrooms and attending trails, watching the other attorneys argue their cases and observing how the judge handled a court room. Ms. Hanford was fascinated, but just didn't feel ready to practice law herself, that is until one evening while visiting night court. A Greek immigrant was brought before the judge without the benefit of a lawyer. The judge heard the charges and then asked the man who his lawyer was. The man didn't have one. The judge started looking around the room for a lawyer who wasn't busy or waiting for his turn. There were none. Then he spotted the young Ms. Hanford and said, "Who are you?" She introduced herself. The judge said, "Are you a lawyer?" She said she was, but was not ready to practice as yet. "Are you a member of the bar?" the judge barked. "Yes" she replied, but I'm not ready," she protested once more. "If you're a member of the bar, you're ready!" said the judge. And that was how it all started. The Greek man was accused of harassing a lion at the zoo. The zoo keepers testified, the vet testified, and all said that the man was bothering the lion. It looked pretty grim for Ms. Hanford's first case, but that's when she made a rather brilliant argument. How did these experts know if her client was actually bothering the lion, she asked. The keepers didn't bring the lion to court so that he could testify. Her client may have been playing with the lion, and after all lions do play pretty rough. Well, that was good enough for the Judge. Case dismissed! She had won her first case! She made a practice of winning cases and for the next few years the talented young woman spent her time and talents defending those with no money, no resources and no ability to defend themselves. She has gone on to do many other things to help people in her life. *It's a Little Known Fact* that young Elizabeth Hanford was one of the staunch defenders of the poor and defenseless, and before she's done, she'll do a lot more. She married well too, to a US Senator and one time Presidential candidate, which is when she changed her name to Elizabeth Dole.

Chaz Allen

Signal Flares

There is no telling how many lives they have saved, or how many lives have been lost because of them. For a long time the military, especially the Navy, used more of them than anyone else. When it came to finding something in the expansive black waters of the ocean at night, nothing was more effective than a signal flare. One shot from a signal flare gun could give someone a message, or an area the size of a football stadium could be flooded with light. The annals of maritime history are filled with the stories of how just being able to see has saved hundreds of lives. They used them to help rescue passengers from the Titanic, hundreds of sailors, downed pilots and even a few lost fisherman. But they have also had their tactical use. During the Civil War, the North had them and the South did not. So, when shooting or trouble started up during the night, a flare was shot over the Confederate Army's head, and

118

suddenly the cover of darkness was no more. The North had a distinct advantage. During World Wars I and II, both sides had them, and again, they were both very useful and very dangerous. Even with all the technology of today, they still make signal flares and use them for any number of occasions. Who came up with the idea of signal flares? Did the U.S. Navy commission a scientist or inventor to come up with this great communication device? Did he work day after day to get it done? Well, that's not what happened. It was a fella by the name of Benjamin Coston of Philadelphia. He was the first to come up with the idea, but he wasn't the first to make them. He tried and he tried hard. He actually worked for several years trying to make his idea work. But, it didn't happen for Benjamin. He took fever and died before he could ever make his first workable flare. But he did leave some good notes. Good enough for another enterprising person to pick up where he left off and eventually make it work out. That probably would have been fine with Ben, for he left something else behind too, and that was a young wife of only 21 years named Martha and 3 tiny children. A 21 year old widow, with three kids, no job, no husband, no skill and no money. Martha may have been alone, broke and down on her luck, but she wasn't dumb. Not by a long shot. ***It's a Little Known Fact*** that when cleaning up Ben's workshop, she found his notes and started working on his ideas herself, with one difference. She made them work. Yes. Martha Coston, a 21 year old destitute widow developed the flares, and sold them to the U.S. Navy to feed her family.

First Movie Star

By 1915, Florence Lawrence had become the world's first movie star. But she was about to do something no one expected. Legendary movie maker D.W. Griffith had started the Biograph Movie Company, and he made Florence the star of all his movies. But one thing was a bit strange. Griffith didn't give Flo any screen credit. So to audiences she didn't have a name. She was simply known as "The Biograph Girl." A little later a tiny little woman named Mary Pickford would become Griffith's star and claim the title of Biograph Girl—but only because Florence had left to work for another movie maker who promised to give Flo the title credits she deserved. Griffith's rival Carl Laemmle realized that audiences didn't necessarily like the Biograph movies as such, they just liked Florence! So Carl offered Florence more money and lured her to his new company, giving her screen credit in the process and publicizing her as his star. To make sure everyone was talking about Florence, Carl even put out a phony story that Florence Lawrence, the Biograph Girl, had tragically died while visiting St. Louis. It wasn't true of course, but movie fans were stunned. Then Carl put out an even bigger story refuting the first story—Florence Lawrence Lives! He then sponsored a public appearance by Florence in St. Louis to prove she was still alive. Thousands turned out to see Florence—nearly doubling the amount of people who had turned out to see President Woodrow Wilson when he visited the city a week earlier. Florence continued to act in Carl's movies and became a true movie star as her name became a household word. It wasn't just publicity that made Florence a star. She was a star in every sense of the word. She was beautiful, and she had a super screen presence, and a sense of energy that even the early silent movies captured. Most people didn't realize, though, that under her beautiful face was a very intelligent and inquisitive mind. She loved to tinker with things, especially mechanical things. The biggest mechanical marvel of her day was the automobile. One thing she realized about early automobiles was that drivers never really knew what other drivers were going to do. They would turn and stop and back up without warning. That caused both a great deal of frustration, accidents and traffic jams. So she decided to do something about it. She invented a couple of little devices that have literally changed driving forever. Florence Lawrence may not be remembered as the world's first movie star who acted in over 275 movies, but ***It's a Little Known Fact*** that everyone knows and uses her invention everyday. Florence Lawrence the movie star invented the automobile turn signals and break signals.

Chaz Allen

Little Dutch Boy

Many remember the story of the Little Dutch Boy but do not remember his name. It's what he did that is remembered. As the story goes, he was walking home from school one day when he noticed a leak in the dyke. Most of Holland is below sea level and is some of the richest farm land in the Netherlands. It's a vital and important part of their economy. There are several towns built on the land, giving farmers easy access to the rich soil. In order to protect the land and the towns, the residents built a system of dykes to keep the salt water out and keep the sea from flooding the towns. It's a good system and has worked for years. But the young hero noticed a problem. There was a leak in one of the main dykes, and if it were to give way the town of Haarlem would be completely destroyed from the flooding sea waters. He knew that something had to be done soon. So, he stuck his finger in the dyke and stopped the leak. This happened to be on a remote part of the dyke and not one that was traveled very often. He had to stand there for quite a while, overnight in fact, until people came to look for him and discovered that not only was he safe, but he had saved the town. Today in the town of Haarlem stands a wonderful little statue commemorating his historic deed. There's just one problem...it never happened! The whole story is a fairly tale made up by an American! Mary Mapes Dodge wrote the story in 1865 in her book "Hans Brinker" or "The Silver Skates". It's from that book that the legend began. There was no little Dutch boy and no hole in the dyke. Then why is there a statue on the site commemorating the historic deed? *It's a Little Known Fact* that so many Americans traveled to the Netherlands and asked to see where the famous event happened that in 1950 the town of Haarlem built the statue to perpetuate their fledgling tourist industry.

First Reporter

Upton Sinclair and Woodward and Bernstein are what we call investigative journalists, and over the last century they've become an important part of American culture. But history might not have remembered them if it weren't for E.C. One of fifteen children in a Pennsylvania family, E.C. left home at a young age to find factory work. But factory jobs only went to certain kinds of people and were closed to everyone else. If anyone outside the "club" did manage to get a factory job, they weren't paid as well as the others, even when they did the same work. This made E.C. angry enough to write to the editors of all the local newspapers. Many articles followed about the factory workers and the unfair, slanted state laws. But it took moving to New York for E.C. to really make an impression. One newspaper editor told E.C.: "If you really want to be a journalist, write about the treatment of the mentally ill." Well, of course he thought he'd seen the last of E.C. But that wasn't the case. E.C. was determined, fooling dozens of doctors and nurses, and even other reporters. E.C. went undercover and was committed to the notorious Blackwell Island Insane Asylum. The horrors were unbelievable. The asylum fed the patients rotten food, allowed them very little sleep, and then made them do all the clean-up work. The nurses dressed the women patients up in comical dresses and made fun of them. They were only bathed once a week or so, and even then the patients were forced to bathe one another in the same water. E.C.'s articles exposed it all. The governor of New York appointed a commission to study the treatment of the mentally ill, and within a few months the legislature had passed new laws forbidding such treatment. This young journalist, barely twenty years old, became America's very first investigative reporter. But people still didn't recognize the name. E.C.'s name did go down in history, though, years later. That's when she -yes, she -decided to test author Jules Verne's theory and see if it was possible to go around the world in eighty days. She did it in seventy-two. ***It's a Little Known Fact*** that E.C. was Elizabeth Cochran, the founder of investigative reporting in America. But she is better known as the globe-trotting adventurer who went by the name of Nellie Bly.

The Toothache

This just wouldn't do! The star had a toothache and she had a performance that night. Lillie Langtry may not be the toast of New York as she once was, but she still had fans and she could still draw an audience. But she wasn't going to do anything unless she had that tooth fixed. This all happen at the turn of the 20th Century before Novicane and precision dental instruments were invented. Going to the dentist meant pain! One of the stage hands suggested she go to a dentist that he had heard of who told stories to his patients while he worked on them. The stories were often so interesting that the patient would sometimes not notice how much pain they were in. It was worth a try. So, she went. The young dentist recognized Ms. Lantry right away, for she was rather famous. She asked him if he was going to tell her a story while he worked on her teeth. The dentist agreed and offered her stories of fishing, baseball and tales of the West.

The dentist had played amateur baseball in his younger days and was a rather accomplished fisherman, too. Ms. Langtry mentioned that she had an admirer in Texas who went by the name of Judge Roy Bean. He had written hundreds of letters to the star, and she was even thinking about stopping in to meet the Judge on her next tour. She thought a story of the Wild West would be nice while the dentist worked on her tooth. And that's just what he did! Soon the talented young dentist had Miss Lilly spellbound with one of his stories. It was so interesting and his delivery so engaging that the star nearly forgot how much it hurt to have a tooth fixed. The patient was verbally carried off to a racing stagecoach being chased by bandits and wild Indians. When it was over she asked the doctor if he ever thought of putting some of his fascinating stories on paper so other people could enjoy them. In fact, he had thought of it. Writing was his secret passion. He really never wanted to be a dentist at all, he confessed. He did it at his father's urging. Other people had told him the same thing, but now he had a big star urging him to do it. And that was enough for Pearl. Yeah, that was his name: Pearl! ***It's a Little Known Fact*** that it was a visit by one time star Lillie Langtry that made him give up dentistry and turn to writing. Millions of fans have been grateful ever since. Most have read the stories of this one time reluctant dentist, accomplished fisherman and amateur baseball player turned world famous author: Pearl Zane Grey!

When Jane Met Ben

It was love at first sight when Jane Sheeny met Ben. He was a tall, gangly fellow with a horsey lope that made her smile. And he was an athlete. He was still wearing the gold medal he had won as a member of the rowing team at the Olympics in Paris. But Ben was somewhat of an unsophisticated big guy who allowed and relied on Jane to introduce him to the world of artists and intellectuals. They made a good team, and soon married and moved to New York City. While Ben was surprising everyone, including himself, by graduating first in his class from medical school, Jane was busy getting to know the writers and academics who hung around Greenwich Village back in the twenties. Ben set up his medical practice and earned quite a reputation as the best in his field. He became well known in New York City as a doctor that many families relied upon for the latest in the new treatments. Ben never stopped learning. He continued to be fascinated by the advancements in medicine, both physical and intellectual. Jane used to tease him about all the time he spent reading about a doctor from Europe who was causing all the talk -a Dr. Sigmund Freud. Well, Ben and Jane decided to start a family. Their first attempts brought pain and sadness when Jane lost their first child early in her pregnancy. Their summertime retreats to a lake in Maine turned out to be the perfect escape where they could help each other deal with the disappointment. It was also the perfect place for Ben to start working on a book that a publisher in New York had asked him to write. They had come to him because of his popular reputation and because of some of the new ideas he had, a lot of which he was basing on his studies of Freud. They turned out to be quite a good team. Ben would narrate his ideas to Jane, who would do more than just type them up. Because she had been through the loss of a child and knew the feelings of a mother, she re-wrote a lot of Ben's terse medical advice into a friendlier, easier language that parents could relate to. *It's a*

Little Known Fact that had it not been for Jane's warm tender writing style, one of the best-selling books of all time might never have been taken off the shelf. The book that almost every family in America owned in the mid twentieth century: "Baby and Child Care," authored by her husband, Dr. Benjamin Spock, but written by Jane Spock.

Martha Jane

It is known that women of the 1850's and 60's did not have the same opportunities as men. In some places they still do not. The young women who weren't satisfied with the traditional roles they were offered often had to take drastic action. Some women did then what some do today: they protested and whined about their situation. But others did take action. They didn't just sit around and talk and write a few protest letters. They went out and got what they wanted from life. That was the case with Martha Jane. She was something of a free spirit, to say the least. She was almost always offended by the gender barriers that society put up, and she was always fighting them. But her way of fighting was to go and prove that she could do anything. Martha Jane was a bit of a tomboy to begin with. She could ride a horse as well as any man, and was a crack shot with a Remington rife. That was her favorite, the Remington. When she heard that the Trans-Continental Railroad was hiring and paying some of the highest wages in the territory, she decided she wanted the job. It was hard, backbreaking work, but no matter. What did matter was that the only job they offered her was as a cook or doing laundry for the men. Oh no! Not Martha! She decided that it was time for a little chicanery. She disguised herself as a man and went and applied for the job. They hired her! For several weeks she worked right along with the men, shoulder to shoulder. No one was the wiser. Everyone thought that Martha was Marty, a baby faced boy that worked as hard as the rest. No telling how long this would have gone on, except for small incident that happened one a hot afternoon. The men had been working on laying rail for several hours. The afternoon temperature had to have been in the 90's. It was a scorcher! The path of the tracks took them right by a lovely cool mountain lake. Needless to say, all the men stripped off their clothes and jumped in. Martha couldn't resist the lure of the cool water. She stripped to her birthday suit and jumped in the water.

It raised more than a few eyebrows. She was discovered and was fired. Silly, isn't it? She had been doing the same work as the men for weeks. But it was against rules. She was out of there, and all because of a brief lapse in judgement and an irresistible cool mountain lake. But that was what most of Martha's life consisted of -lapses in judgement of one kind or another, or just lying. She had more than one embarrassing moment in her life and told more than one whopper of a tale. That's pretty much how she got her name. Not Martha Jane -that was the one her parents gave her. Wild Bill Hickok gave her the nickname. ***It's a Little Known Fact*** that Martha Jane Cannary, the woman who disguised herself to work as a man and who was so prone to errors of judgement, became know for just that ... calamities ...Calamity Jane!

Her Knight In Shining Armor

All Sarah knew was that she was in love. Like most young women her age, she had dreamed that her knight in shining armor would ride up and rescue her, but there was a problem. Oh, she had found her knight all right! His name was Jeff. Sarah loved him, and Jeff loved her. They wanted to be married. Jeff had even asked her father for Sarah's hand in marriage. That took a lot of courage, for Sarah's father was Zachary Taylor, the man who would become President. Even then, he was a general in the Army and on the fast track to the White House. Jeff was a lieutenant in Taylor's command. The marriage should have been a sure thing. But her father had said no, and that was a problem. General Taylor led American forces against Mexico during the Mexican American War. One of the officers under his command was Jeff. Taylor didn't think much of Davis as a solider or an officer. Evidently that was enough to stop a wedding. But head strong Sarah did it anyway. Sarah defied her father and married Jeff, becoming estranged from her family in the process. Most would hope that Sarah and Jeff lived happily ever after. But they didn't! The beautiful young Sarah, who had turned her back on her father and her entire family, died from malaria only three months after the wedding. But that wasn't the end of Zachary Taylor and the young Jeff's relationship. At the Battle of Monterey, Taylor saw Jeff in battle, leading a regiment of volunteers. Jeff fought intelligently and valiantly. General Taylor realized what a fine leader Jeff was. The victory at Monterey turned Zachary Taylor into a highly-touted Presidential candidate. He owed much of his popularity to Jeff. A few months later, young Jeff was badly wounded in the Battle of Buena Vista. General Zachary Taylor personally saw to his care. As Jeff recuperated from his wounds, the soon to be President was heard to say, "My daughter was a better judge of men than I." After the war, Taylor became President and the two men became even closer friends. The two families often celebrated holidays together, and Jeff was a frequent visitor to the White House. ***It's a Little Known Fact*** that years earlier, Zachary Taylor had forbidden his daughter from marrying the man of her dreams, but she did it anyway. Who knows what might have happened if Taylor had given his daughter permission to marry the next President. Yes, President! Not of the United States, but of the Confederacy. Sarah became Mrs. Jefferson Davis.

A Love Story?

It's the oldest story in the world...for the love of a woman. The woman in this story was Peggy Shippen. It really didn't matter who you asked, the answer was always the same. If the question was who was the most beautiful and most popular person in Philadelphia in the late 1770's, the response was the lovely Peggy Shippen. There was no question, Peggy was the belle of the ball. Any ball, any time. The men of the day described her as being of exquisite charm and alarming beauty. Peggy was the 19 year old daughter of a Philadelphia doctor, and she was popular. She lived the lifestyle of a wealthy doctor's daughter. Extravagant would be the right word here. When the Continental Congress convened, she was courted by some of the most famous men in the colonies. Later, when the British Army overran Philadelphia, she was courted by no less than the General's staff. Peggy herself had no real loyalties.

Her father had made much of his wealth from trade with the England and really didn't treasure the idea of being cut off from their source of money. When the General Washington and the American troops finally did run the Brits out of Philadelphia and recaptured the town, Peggy was right in the middle of the whole thing welcoming the conquering troops back. But there was a problem. Her father's British leanings were no longer welcome, and as a result he was going broke fast under the new Colonial rule. That was a disaster for Peggy. She had to find a husband who could support her in the lifestyle she had grown accustomed too, and she did: an American General who was a battle field hero with a brilliant future and a man who was completely and total memorized by the beautiful Miss Shippen. They were married, and Peggy went right on spending and throwing parties and buying, until even the General's purse was strained to the max. The hero was going in debt with no hope of recovery. He knew he couldn't go on this way. Something had to be done. The last thing he would consider is giving up the most beautiful woman he had ever seen. His love and infatuation for Peggy was more than he could stand, so he made a deal that would seal his fate forever. He made a deal for 20,000 pounds Sterling to surrender West Point. But fortunately, it didn't happen! His plan was discovered before he could do it. He and his bride were forced to flee America and spend the rest of their lives in England, there dying in near poverty. The General is remembered to this day, but almost no one remembers the reason he did what he did. *It's a Little Known Fact* that it was the General's misplaced devotion to the one time belle of the ball Peggy Shippen that caused Benedict Arnold to do what he did.

The Songwriter

There was one thing everyone agreed on: Lydia was a beautiful young woman. And she could write a beautiful melody. Her songs were so good, they were recorded by such stars as Elvis Presley, Bing Crosby and Andy Williams. Over 500 singers in all have recorded Lydia's songs. And yet most people don't know that Lydia was a songwriter. Her life was so wrapped up in other things that her musical talent was rarely mentioned. Lydia was born in 1838. When she was a little girl, she attended what was called "the Royal School". It was there that she developed her skill of composing beautiful songs. In her lifetime she would write over 200 songs, including one of the national anthems of her country. When Lydia was 24 she married John. Life was filled with wonderful, happy, peaceful days until fate dealt Lydia a double blow. Her brother David died in 1891 and she had to take over his responsibilities. It was hard enough to take on so much new responsibility, but the death of her husband John just a few months later made it much worse. Perhaps that is why you hear sadness in the words to many of her famous songs. She continued to write poems and songs throughout her life, which was a life filled with danger, disappointment and responsibility. Lydia wanted her homeland to belong to her people, the ones who had lived there for hundreds of years before strangers arrived from both the west and the east. When she took over, she decided that her country was going to be ruled by her and her people, not by faceless corporations. Well, the corporation big shots would hear none of that and they simply called the President of the United States, who sent in the Marines and placed Lydia under house arrest for eight months. She finally gave in so that her supporters could be released from prison. She wrote her most famous song about the sad farewell between two lovers, but most people interpret it to be her own sad goodbye to her country. ***It's a Little Known Fact*** that Lydia was the last queen of Hawaii. Her full name was Lydia Paki Kamekeha Liliuokalani. And that famous song which translates to "Farewell to Thee"? You probably know it better as "Aloha Oe".

The Beautiful Mexican

The crowd in Tijuana watching the young dancer called her "the beautiful Mexican." She could dance beautifully. Even at 15 years old, she could hold her own with the best. She came by it naturally. Her father Edwardo Cansino was a dancer, and he had taught Margarita. Now, the student was upstaging the teacher, as so often happens. It was Margarita's turn to shine and she was doing very well. It may have been just a little cantina in Tijuana, but to Margarita it was as good as the Hollywood Bowl. She was performing! She knew that she was going to be famous. She said so often. And the time was right. There were very few Hispanic stars in the 1930's, but Margarita and her father really didn't see that as a problem. It was time for one, and Margarita was ready to take the lead. Even a top Hollywood talent scout like Winfield Sheenan thought so. Those were his very thoughts as he sat and watched the lovely young Mexican woman dance that night in Tijuana. She was beautiful and she was Mexican. Well, almost. She was beautiful, very beautiful, but she wasn't Mexican. She was of Spanish descent. Her father was from an aristocratic family in Spain. Her mother was a direct descendent of the Pilgrims who settled around Boston. So Margarita was Hispanic alright, but not Mexican. Would that be a problem? The talent scout for Warner Brothers didn't know, but he knew talent when he saw it and he knew star quality. So he made arrangements for her to appear in a bit part in a movie staring the Brazilian bombshell Delores del Rio. Her father got a walk on part, too. So it was that the beautiful young Mexican girl came to Hollywood to make a name for herself. The young woman went on to become one of Hollywood's biggest and most glamours stars. She caught the attention of such mega stars as Victor Mature and Georgie Jessel, Gary Merrill and Glen Ford, all of whom proposed marriage. She said no. Orson Wells who also asked, and she said yes. Most people have heard of her and seen her in a dozen movies and thousands of magazines. But most don't know that she was this country's first 'Hispanic' superstar. That little tag of "the beautiful Mexican," seems to have been left behind. ***It's a Little Known Fact*** that Margarita Cansino, daughter of Edwardo and Volva Cansino, took her mother's maiden name for her own and was in fact this country's first Hispanic superstar. She will always be remembered as the beautiful Rita Hayworth!

Fashion Statement

Every spring when the new line of fashions comes out, all the great designers put on such a show of their new designs and bring out an entire line of new clothes. Only the very lucky, or very rich, or those who work for the right fashion magazine are invited to the big shows. They can be seen on television, with fabulous looking models, every one pencil thin, walking down the runway in front of a group of admiring buyers and photographers. If the designer has a successful show, then their season is made and they will have a good year. If their new designs and styles don't impress the elite, then it could be a very rough year for them. So, needless to say, each one tries to put on a good show. Often, fashion trends follow, and women everywhere begin buying the new styles or at least the knock offs at the local department store. There is no question that the talented designers have had a profound impact on the way Americans live and dress. One designer had more of an impact on American fashion than anyone else. She had more influence on the way the world dresses than any other single individual. Who was it? Most know the really big names, such as Donna Karen, Bill Blass, Gucci, Ralph Lauren, Nicole Miller. Each has had a significant impact on fashion world wide, but none as much as Clare. When Clare designed a dress, it was immediately copied by dozens of manufacturers and sent to the stores at near lighting speed. One fashion editor once said that "if she threw a scarf around someone's waist, a million women would be wearing them tomorrow." Another said, "I know of no one who has had a more profound impact on what women of the world wear than her." And the funny part is that Clare never meant to do it. She wasn't a fashion designer, at least not the kind normally thought of. She never sold a dress in a store. She never designed anything for the fashion industry. She never hired a model in her life. That just wasn't for Clare. She was just doing her job. And she did it very well, probably better than anyone else has ever done it. All she was doing was trying to make someone look good. And even more importantly, look right for the part. And when she did, millions of men and women watched and copied her ideas. ***It's a Little Known Fact*** that Clare has more designs copied and manufactured than any other designer in the world. How was this done? Well, it's when the public saw her designs in such films as Holiday Inn, For Whom the Bell Tolls, Beau Geste, Sunset Boulevard, A Place in the Sun and a over 1000 other movies. She is the 35 time Oscar Nominated costume designer to the movies Edith Clare Head.

The Print Shop

It was a print shop. In appearance it was not unlike most others. It had a printing press, one that was imported from England, all the letters and numbers, which in those days were made if brass, and of course ink. That was basically it! There were a few more things here and there around the shop, but that was the biggest part of what was need to do the printing. But this print shop was special for two reasons. First, it was the Glover Print Shop, and the Glover Print Shop was the very first printer to establish in America. Second, it was the only print shop. So it befell this shop to print virtually everything that was to be printed at the time. This was during the 1600s, and printing was done a bit differently than it is now. First someone had to write what ever was going to be printed and that was done in long hand with quill and ink. Next it had to be typeset one letter at a time with heavy brass letters, upside down and backwards so it could be transferred directly onto the paper. That was a skill in itself. They used brass letters so they would stand up to the big heavy press coming down on them time after time. Then of course came the laborious process of making enough copies, one by one, for everyone who wanted to read what was being printed. Last they had to be cut up, edges trimmed, folded and packaged. And all this took place by hand! Since the Glover shop was the first print shop in America, it had to do all it could to supply the community. It produced business forms, Almanacs, flyers, brochures, even prayer books and hymnals for the churches. Not to mention a weekly newspaper. For each and every one, they had to go through the same process of doing everything by hand. But they did. The Glover Print Shop was not only the first print shop, it was also one of the most successful. Well, it was right after the local townsfolk got over who was running it. That's right, at first the Glover Print Shop didn't do too well. People thought it was unseemly. But after the weekly newspaper started coming out and people realized that it was their best source for news from both home and abroad, and that it was well written and interesting, things started to smooth out a bit. Business increased and the little print shop went down in history for two reasons. First, it was the first print shop, and second because of it's owner/operator. ***It's a Little Known Fact*** that the first print shop in America was owned and operated by Mistress Glover, a widow woman who set the standard of work so high that it was 31 years before a second print shop could successfully compete. Good for her!

Phoebe

It was a hot August day when Phoebe was born. It was on a small farm in northern Ohio in 1860 when Mrs. Mosey gave birth to her fifth daughter. The farm itself never provided the Moseys with a comfortable living, but Phoebe's father Jacob was an expert hunter, and he more than managed to keep his family well-fed by hunting game in the surrounding woods. But that all changed when Phoebe was just five years old: Jacob died suddenly, leaving no one to support the family. Little Phoebe missed her daddy, and she would often sit for hours and stare at Jacob's hunting rifle hung idly above the fireplace. She would remember happier times when she used to accompany him on hunting trips to bring home supper, days vastly different from the ones she was experiencing now. The situation for the Mosey family was deteriorating rapidly. Phoebe's mother was forced to sell the farm and all of the animals just to feed her family. And one by one their resources dwindled until the family was facing the possibility of real hunger. Somebody had to do something quick. And so it was that Phoebe, now eight years old, made a bold move. She took her father's old hunting rifle down from where it had hung above the fireplace. She snuck it out of the house and into the woods to hunt for game the way she'd seen her father do when she was just five years old. She was no expert, that's for sure, and she was so bad that the butt of the rifle broke her nose the first time she fired it. Phoebe came home with two things that day -a bloody nose and dinner for the family. But the family situation steadily worsened and her mother was forced to split the family up. Phoebe was sent to live with a farmer and his wife who needed a girl to work for them. Phoebe's day began at 4 a.m and didn't end until 10pm at night. For three years the old couple nearly worked her to death. But when she learned that they had reneged on their promise to pay her mother 50 cents a week for her service, that was the last straw, and she left them in the middle of the night. Now 15, she began hunting and trapping game again and selling it to local hotels and restaurants in northern Ohio. She became such an accurate shot and so prolific that she not only paid off the mortgage on her family's farm but also started a career that would take her to perform for kings and presidents alike the world over. ***It's a Little Known Fact*** that the noted "Wild West" markswoman who was born and raised a little eastern farm girl, and who learned to shoot to feed her family was none other than the legendary Annie Oakley.

Brooklyn Bridge

Most have heard the old adage, "If you believe that, I've got a bridge I'd like to sell you!" The bridge is the famed Brooklyn Bridge, which spans the East River from Manhattan to Brooklyn in New York City. It was one of the first suspensions bridges. They call it a hybrid with cable stays and gravity anchored. Not only is it used for automobile traffic, but also light railroad and pedestrians. When it opened in May of 1883, it was called a marvel of engineering and today it is still an impressive sight. Thousands of people who visit New York each year make sure that a trip to the Brooklyn Bridge is on their agenda. Washington A. Roebling was the chief engineer on the bridge and it was supposed to be the crowning achievement in his professional career. It was, at least to a certain extent. But another person actually deserves more credit than Roebling. Roebling couldn't finish the job. In fact, he barely got it started. When they were setting the caisson, the foundation for the bridge which was 78 feet underwater, Roebling became ill, quite ill. It was decompression sickness. Very little was known about it then. The horrible illness left the brilliant engineer paralyzed, partly blind, deaf and mute. Not a good situation with such a huge undertaking as the Brooklyn Bridge on his plate. Roebling couldn't work and no one else was willing to take on the awesome responsibilities of the job. Except one person. One who knew almost nothing of construction or engineering. One who didn't even know higher math. One who had only a deep belief in Roebling's work. It wasn't easy. It was a job that would have challenged the top engineers of the time, much less a laymen. But that didn't stop someone who was committed. It required learning higher math and engineering on the job. It required being a conduit between engineering and construction. It required learning some of the most difficult construction methods ever accomplished at that time. It required a lot. *It's a Little Known Fact* that if it hadn't been for the dedication of the person

160

who was willing to take over as surrogate chief engineer, there may not have been a Brooklyn bridge. So, thank her! Yes her! Emily Roebling, the very smart and talented wife of Washington Roebling, is the primary reason that famous bridge stands today.

Chaz Allen

The Team

It was one of the most successful sports franchises ever put together. It lasted 60 years, longer than most franchises. They won over 85% of their games against some of the toughest teams in the world. They didn't just play in America. They played in the Philippines, much of Europe and Asia, and all of America, of course. They were a basketball team, a very special kind of team. They had some outstanding players, such as Butch Moore, who scored 35,426 points in just 11 seasons. Or Red Mason, who not only was an outstanding player during the regular game, but during the half time break would sit down at half court and proceed to sink 25 baskets in a row from that position. They traveled to Hollywood on several occasions and had a little fun with some of the stars on the court, like Henry Fonda, William Holden, Tyrone Power and Bing Crosby. But that was for fun. When another professional team was on the court, they were all business. They were the first to come up with a number of shots that are very popular today with many of the NBA and WNBA teams, like the alley-oop, the reverse dunk, and the air-pass. But they don't get the credit for those because they weren't a members of the NBA and none of their games were televised. And not everyone wanted to see them play. They were different than the basketball teams of the time. They didn't fit. They looked different and they dressed different. The owner of the team, Orwell Moore, once said that "there was no question they were discriminated against from the beginning because of their color." The thing that was the most remarkable was their stamina. When half time came and the opposing team went to the locker room to catch their breath, these remarkable players stayed on the court and entertained the crowd with their masterful ball handling and trick shots. They never took a break at all! When the other team returned all rested and fresh, it didn't seem to matter, for they lost anyway.

Chaz Allen

What was it that made this so different? Well, they weren't men! ***It's a Little Known Fact*** that a team called The All American Red Heads Basketball Team, which was made up of all women and played by the men's rules against men's teams, toured for more than fifty years and won over 85% of their games. This team did more than anyone else to promote and gain acceptance of women's basketball in America today. And the color discrimination thing that the owner was speaking about? Well, that was because they had all dyed their hair red, of course.

The Teacher

By all accounts, Sam was a remarkable man: a graduate of Harvard Medical School, an active abolitionist, and a reformist for the mentally ill, the mentally retarded, and prisoners. It was in 1821 when Sam volunteered as a soldier and a surgeon in the Greek Revolution, and spent the next few years helping Greece win independence from Turkey. When Sam returned home, he received a proposal to organize an asylum for the blind in Boston. Never one to do things willy-nilly, Sam sailed to Europe to learn more about the subject first. Once he arrived in Europe, though, Sam was diverted again. At the time, Poland was involved in a little matter called the Polish Insurrection, and it looked to Sam like they could use some help. The Prussian government had other ideas, however, and let Sam cool his heels in one of their prisons for a while before allowing him to return to Boston. But even a stint in prison didn't cool his passion. Sam hadn't forgotten why he had traveled to Europe in the first place, and he began working with a few blind children out of his father's house. He quickly became the leading expert on the subject, and in 1832 the Perkins School for the Blind was established, with Sam as its first director. Things were going pretty well for Sam and the Perkins School for the Blind when he read a newspaper article about the life of young Laura Bridgman. Laura was born a perfectly healthy baby girl, but when she was two years old she was struck by scarlett fever. The disease destroyed her hearing, her sight, and left her with little sense of smell or taste. The only sense Laura had left was her sense of touch. Laura simply followed her mother around, clinging to an old boot for comfort. Now in those days there really wasn't anything you could do for a child in such as Laura, but Sam thought if the damage from the disease couldn't be fixed, he could at least teach the girl to handle life. He brought Laura to the Perkins Institute and placed raised letters on everyday things, such as plates and spoons. Laura learned to match the raised letters with the objects and eventually understood that she could take an idea from her mind and convey it to another. Laura learned to write using grooved paper, later writing both poetry and an autobiography. Laura may have been the first to receive benefit from Sam's wonderful training and innovation, and she certainly wasn't the last: so did Anne Sullivan! ***It's a Little Known Fact*** that had it not been for Sam Howe, there probably would never have been an Anne Sullivan, and you might recall that Anne Sullivan was Helen Keller's teacher.

Alice The Sculptor

It seems like the two have almost always been opposed to each other. Not in a hostile way, but in their basic goals and objectives; one for pleasure, one for progress. But sometimes art and science can come together in such a way as to further one or the other by enormous leaps. That was the case with Alice. She was an artist, a sculptor. She lived and worked in Dayton, Ohio, and she loved to make things with her hands. Alice saw beauty in so many things and it was her life's desire to put that beauty into a form to be enjoyed by most everyone. Art has so many facets, and sculpting is just one of them, but it is one of the most enduring. The great statues have endured through the centuries, such as the famed Pieta at the Vatican, or Michelangelo's David, or the Goddess Venus in the Louve. Even the Statue of Liberty is a testament to both the art itself and the lasting friendship of the people who made it. Alice felt all of that when she sculpted. She was aware of the lasting contributions she was making to society, to art, to progress. Progress?? Well, yes progress, because in this case art and science came together to help give mankind a boost in another way. The Air Force was conducting rather secret research. It had been going on for some time and they felt as if they were getting close to a really big breakthrough. The scientists knew that if they could accomplish this task, so much would change. The whole system from the nations defense to progress in the frontiers of science would change with this one accomplishment. So it was a top priority. But as with most things radically new, more than just the idea had to be developed. They also had to develop new equipment and use new science to accomplish their great goal. The equipment they had at the time was good enough for past uses, but not for this. This would take something new, bold and unique. That's when the Air Force turned to Alice the sculptor and asked her to come up with what was needed. The Air Force had some rather stringent and detailed specifications alright, but that was the challenge. She must design the new piece of equipment to not only meet the Air Force's strict requirements, but also it had to fit comfortably. Yes, fit. Someone had to wear it. And someone did. The goal was accomplished, and everything did change. ***It's a Little Known Fact*** that a sculptor from Dayton, Ohio, named Alice King Chatham was responsible for designing the very helmet that Chuck Yeager needed to fly the X-15 and break the sound barrier for the first time. It's not like the Air Force to let a good thing go. Alice went on to later design the very helmets that the brave Astronauts wear to this very day. That is definitely a successful blending of art and science.

The First Trip

As an engineering student, Karl Benz studied steam engines. The steam engine was a driving force of the machine age, invented in the early 1700s. In 1864, when Karl graduated from college, he went to work as an engineer, working thirteen hour days in a large factory that produced railway locomotives. It was hard, dirty work but he stuck with it until fortune brought young Berta Ringer his way. In 1872 the couple was married, and with a little help from Berta, Karl set up a shop of his own, a small concern that failed to thrive as the little family added two sons to the list of mouths to feed. But eventually, after a lot of hard work and patience, Karl had a breakthrough. He successfully designed a small engine that met some enthusiasm from the public, and by the time Berta had given birth to two more children, Karl had established himself as a moderately successful producer of engines. Financially stable at last, Karl turned his attention to bigger and better things. What he had in mind was to put his engine to work as part of something the world had never seen before: a motor vehicle. Most will have guessed by now that Karl was the inventor of one of the first automobiles -a far cry from the upscale vehicles that today bear the name Mercedes-Benz. This contraption looked like a cross between a bicycle and a riding mower, and ran just under 8 miles per hour over a distance of around a half a mile. Despite the machine's modest appearance, Karl's automobile created a local sensation. Crowds gathered to watch it approach. One old woman fled indoors, convinced that Benz was the devil driving an infernal carriage. To escape all the public attention. Karl began running his test drives at night. Perhaps he was the shy type, but there was another member of the Benz family who understood that there's no such thing as bad publicity. Karl's wife Berta may have been the one to suggest that Karl offer his automobile for public sale. He was the first inventor to do so. In any case, she never failed to stand by her husband's side, even as the newspapers condemned the new vehicle, calling it "useless...ridiculous...and indecent." Berta, along with a select group of others, didn't share the popular hostility towards the idea of motorized driving. In fact she thought the automobile would be perfect for leisurely weekend trips through the country. Basically, Berta thought that all the automobile needed was a little publicity, a concept car manufacturers rely on to this day. And so one morning in 1888, while her husband was still peacefully asleep, Berta got up and took her sons Eugen and Richard for a little drive to Pforzheim. The roads were dusty, dirty, and full of stones -intended for horses, not cars. Berta carried her own fuel, for there were of course no filling stations. And when she hit a hill, she and Eugen got out and pushed while Richard steered. The other travelers on the road that day may have known that they were witnessing a little piece of history as they watched. Perhaps they were amused as the mother and sons made their dusty way across country. At village after village Berta got help from local merchants, like the cobbler who hammered fresh leather onto a wooden brake block. She used one of her own garters as insulating tape to mend a short circuit in the electrical system and cleared a blocked fuel jet with a hairpin. So for those who make jokes about women drivers, remember this: ***It's a Little Known Fact*** that the first long-distance automobile trip took place with a woman behind the wheel. Berta Benz, wife of auto inventor and tycoon Karl Benz, was the first person to drive a car cross-country -a woman whose husband didn't even know the car had left the garage!

The Shoot-Out

It was just for fun. It was meant to be a publicity photo for an upcoming event, but things were quickly getting out of hand. At least that's what the press agent thought. These two were very competitive, that for sure, and he really should have know better than to put two such strong personalities together, especially with weapons. One was a well known and very talented athlete, and a super shot with a bow and arrow. The other was known for high adventure and daring escapades. Only a few were aware that this person was also a crack pistol shot. When a publicity agent for the adventurer suggested a photo op with the world famous athlete, with each of them having target practice with their weapon of choice, the stage was set for trouble. It started rather simply as the agent later told the story. The athlete took a shot with the bow and arrow and split the target. The world adventurer followed suit. First the bow, then the pistol. Again and again. Evidently it didn't take long for the two to start looking for more interesting and challenging targets to shoot at. They started to wonder off the property where the photos were being taken and headed toward town. Shots were being taken at barns, weather veins on roof tops, hay bales, and a few road signs along the way. It was a pretty good match up. The bow and arrow against a pistol. Neither contestant seemed to have a clear advantage over the other. It didn't take long before the people in town started to notice what was going on, and that two very famous people were shooting it out, so to speak. A crowd started to follow the two around, and even started pointing out more interesting and difficult targets to shoot. The contestants obliged. Neither wanted to give in to the other. Runners were sent back to the house for more arrows and bullets. While they waited, refreshments were served, compliments of a local business. The crowd was growing pretty large when the Sheriff showed up and wanted to know what was going on. He had a couple of reports of two characters shooting up a barn and someone's weather vein. Who was going to pay? His eyes got pretty big when he saw who was doing all the damage. But he had a job to do. The two shooters agreed to pay half each and the Sheriff agreed not to put them in jail for several offenses. But he insisted that it was the end of the so called competition. And it was, much to the disappointment of the rather large crowd. They would never know who was the best between the bow and arrow and the pistol. *It's a Little Known Fact* that two great people almost went to jail over a little friendly competition. One was a great athlete the other a great pilot and adventurer. The athlete was Babe Didrikson Zahorias and the pilot was Amelia Earheart!

Henrietta's Duel

Some women dream about two men fighting to death over them. This happened to Henrietta, and she knew she was the cause of it all. She had a full-time companion and lover, but she was bored with the relationship and started keeping company with another man. Ah, the eternal triangle! Has anything good ever come out of it? It had come to the point where Henrietta was standing in her large dressing room watching two men with swords fight over her. She was an actress. She was one of the best known and most loved actresses in the world during the 1880's and 90's. Her performances on stage captivated the hearts of the thousands who came to see her. More than just a few men dreamed of having Henrietta for themselves. But there was one gentleman who had her attention, and they had been keeping company for some time. In her eyes, he was a brave, handsome, and generous man, although a bit of a prude. In addition to being known as one of the great stage actresses of her day, Henrietta was also something of a political activist. She frequently went public with her beliefs and caused her companion many embarrassing moments. He became the topic of careless talk as a result of her radical views and actions. She was known to pull stunts such as showing up at a political rally in the nude to emphasize a point, something her beau didn't take kindly to at all. He was something of a chauvinist and insisted that Henrietta behave herself. She resented his demands, and in typical Henrietta fashion began flirting with another gentleman to keep the first one in his place. One thing led to another: some warnings were given, some challenges made and accepted, and before long they were fighting with very deadly weapons right in Henrietta's dressing room at the theater. And it was all her doing. She thought herself something of a contradiction, however. All her life she had been an outspoken opponent of the death penalty, yet she found herself thrilled to see two lovers fighting to the death over her. Not only did she not feel bad about causing the duel, she later admitted that she was thrilled by it. The fight seemed even for a while, and then it became obvious that her new suitor was gaining the advantage. Well, that wasn't suppose to happen. She had only toyed with him to make her long-time companion jealous. Suddenly it was over. With one last parry and thrust, her long-time love fell to the floor dead. The new man was victorious. He turned smiling to Henrietta, ready to accept her gratitude. Imagine his shock when he turned and found her rushing at him full steam. Henrietta was so upset that the wrong man had won the duel, she pushed him out of a second story window, nearly killing him. Henrietta continued doing what she did best: performing. She was known throughout 30 countries for her skill and talent on stage, but no one knew about this bit of chicanery. ***It's a Little Known Fact*** that the world's leading actress of the 1880's was also the subject of a duel, and she was responsible for nearly killing the winner, even though she had started the whole thing herself. Who was she? Henrietta Rosine, known to the world as Sarah Burnheardt.

What Didn't Interest The Navy

Richard James had just graduated from college at Penn State as a mechanical engineer when he took his first job was at the shipyard in Philadelphia. The year was 1943 and America was deeply involved in World War II. Richard was on a special "new ship's run" when his ship encountered some rough water, and that's when it struck him. What the Navy needed was a better way to hold a ship's sensitive instruments steady even in stormy seas. Before long he had developed some prototypes that did just that! He showed them to the Navy, but the Navy wasn't interested. One day while he was tinkering around his shop, he knocked one of his prototypes off of the table and was fascinated at the way it acted. He took the device home to his wife Betty and asked her if she thought he might be able to sell it as a toy instead. Betty liked the idea, so over the next two years, Richard experimented to find the perfect the toy. They got a patent in 1945, and with 500 dollars which he had to borrow, made 400 prototypes. But the trouble was, the toy didn't look like much when it was sitting on the store shelves and nobody was buying. Christmas was fast approaching and it was make or break time for Richard and Betty and their toy. Finally a sympathetic toy buyer at Gimbel's department store in Philadelphia gave them permission to put on an in-store demonstration at the far corner of the toy department. Richard and Betty were so afraid that nobody would buy their toy that they asked a friend to act as a shill. They even had to give him the necessary $1 so he could buy one and perhaps attract others. But the shill wasn't necessary. They were mobbed. Customers came from all over the store to see the funny new toy, and within minutes all 400 were sold. Richard's unique toy was a hit and it continued to grow in popularity. But success was apparently not enough for Richard James, whose story took an unexpected turn in 1960 when he suddenly left his family and moved to Bolivia to join a religious sect.

He left Betty alone with their six children and a load of debt he incurred by giving their money to his new friends. Betty relocated the factory to her hometown in Hollidaysburg, Pennsylvania, where it remains today, and she has carried on the tradition she and Richard started so many years ago with the help of family and friends. In the 1960's an aggressive advertising campaign and a catchy jingle helped sales continue to expand. The toy cost $1 when it was introduced in 1945. And even today the price has risen only to $2, although the company generates more than $15 million in revenues annually. There's no research and development department and the little toy looks almost identical to the first one Richard made. It is still so simple that it only takes the factory 10 seconds to make. Yes, 10 seconds and $2 for a toy that has been used more than any other by science teachers for demonstrating properties such as centripetal force and sound and light waves. It is a toy that soldiers in Vietnam slung over trees to make radio antennae. It is a toy that people have used as pigeon repellers, mail holders, drapery tie-backs, pecan pickers and gutter protectors. All in all, 250 million have been sold world wide. And polls have shown that 90 percent of Americans recognize the name of Richard's invention, which was the result of accidentally knocking one of his engineering efforts from a table back in 1943. For what Richard noticed that day was that the thing fell end over end. ***It's a Little Known Fact*** that Richard James' device, which failed to interest the Navy, was a simple spring that became one of the most successful toys of all time, known as the slinky.

Great Chicago Fire

There was one thing people truly feared in the early days of the country's history. Many still fear it today, but it's not the threat that it used to be. What is it that so many people fear? Well, fire! Today, there are brick and concrete buildings, fire retardant materials and clothes, fire suppression systems, sprinkler systems, and much more. Even the fire departments are much better equipped and the personnel are much better trained than ever before. Most sleep better at night because of these wonderful innovations. But that wasn't always the case. Much of the country was built with wood, just about the most flammable material around. It definitely burns well! And that of course was the problem. Almost everything was made out of wood, mostly because it was readily available everywhere and easy to use. But because wood is so flammable, history is littered with hundreds of stories of devastating fires, such as San

Francisco. Most think that an earthquake was the big problem, and an earthquake did cause a lot of damage, but it was the resulting fire that did far more damage. Of course when General Sherman attacked Atlanta, he practically burned the whole city down. Almost no city has been exempt from the fear and results of a huge fire in their community. Perhaps the most famous is the great Chicago fire. That fateful day Mrs. O'Leary's cow kicked over a lantern while she was milking and set fire to the barn. Soon the whole town was in flames, and an enormous part of that great city was leveled by the fire. It took nearly a week to put out. The combination of all the tender cured wooden buildings standing so close to each other and the lack of water pressure and modern fire fighting equipment made it an inferno that has almost never been equaled. What a story! And that's exactly what it was -a story! Oh, the fire happened. Chicago was nearly completely destroyed by that huge fire. But *It's a Little Known Fact* that Mrs. O'Leary's cow had nothing to do with it. The fire started in the middle of the night when

Mrs. O'Leary was in bed sound asleep. The cow was in a dark barn with no lanterns. So how did that famous lie get started? A newspaper reporter! Michael Ahern, a newspaper reporter, admitted later that he made the whole thing up to give the story a better angle. But he admitted his lie only after nearly every newspaper in the country had reprinted the story and took it into history.

Hello Dolley

Few members of Washington, D.C. society can claim to have been loved by all, but when Dolley Madison died in 1849 at the age of eighty-one, she came pretty close. Dolley had been the toast of the town for about a half-century, beginning her reign as "Queen Dolley" as she was called during the Presidency of her husband James. Even after leaving the White House in 1817, Dolley remained one of Washington's star attractions, known for her warm friendly personality, her lavish dinner parties, and her fashion sense which was the envy of all. Long before husband James rose to the Presidency, Dolley had a taste for colorful gowns and elegant trappings and loved to preside over fancy dinner parties and receptions. General George Washington declared her the sprightliest card partner he had ever had, and Abigail Adams prized the invitations she received to dine at Dolley's home. When her husband took his place as Thomas Jefferson's Secretary of State, Dolley moved with him to the center of Washington society and was so adept socially that even Jefferson, well known for his sophistication and taste, invited her to be his hostess for the most important diplomatic affairs. She was known as the Queen of Washington City, and no fashionable Washington lady failed to follow the trends she set in clothing and headwear, like the brightly colored turbans that became her trademark hats. But all was not dinner parties and card games for the charming Dolley. During the War of 1812 a sober mood fell upon Washington. Dolley's natural vivaciousness helped keep morale high in the capitol city, but late in 1814 word reached the President's house that the British had landed in Maryland and were headed for Washington. Madison knew he must leave for the front and urged his wife to escape at once to Virginia while he oversaw the preparations for the capital's defense. But Dolley insisted on staying in Washington until she could be sure her husband was safe, and so Madison rode off leaving his wife alone in the White House. About 1:30 p.m. in the sultry afternoon of a Washington August, Dolley sat down to eat. No sooner had she begun than she heard the roar of cannons in the distance. Rushing out, she called for a carriage, and commandeered a large wagon nearly. Several panicky men soothed by Dolley's reassurances helped her to load precious papers and books from the executive mansion.

Ignoring the pleas of friends whose carriages were pulling hastily out of town, Dolley searched the house for the remaining treasures she knew she must save for the young country. A young lieutenant rode up to the White House door calling that the British were nearby and that she must allow him to get her out of Washington at once. But Dolley refused to go to safety till she had secured one last item. Not long after her carriage finally rolled away, the British invaded Washington, set fire to the President's house and then as a thunderstorm broke, left the city. But not before Dolley saved much of our American history, and one item in particular. It was a painting, one so treasured that she risked death or capture to save it for all generations of Americans. **It's a Little Known Fact** that the portrait every schoolchild knows by heart -the famous Gilbert Stuart portrait of George Washington, the father of our country, was preserved for posterity by the courageous Dollcy Madison.

She Would Be Scarlet

She knew that she was perfect for the part, and what a part it was. It wasn't too often that movie companies came to Georgia to make a movie, so when David O. Selznick brought an entire movie company to town to film Margaret Mitchell's fabulous best seller, Catherine Campbell knew she was right for the role of Scarlet O'Hara. Catherine was a delicate Southern flower, a native of Atlanta who possessed all the charm and grace that the part would demand. She was an experienced actress, having done a number of roles in local Atlanta theater companies. Catherine knew other young Southern belles were vying for the part too, but she was the one. She auditioned for Selznick and watched as the most handsome man in movies in 1939 arrived on the set: Clark Gable to play Rhett Butler. Catherine took one look at Gable and knew she wouldn't have much trouble falling in love with him. Clark was a handsome devil. He was as big off the screen as he was on. He was one of the few who deserved the title of movie legend. And he was a fine man. Catherine also watched as the talented English actor Leslie Howard arrived to play the part of Ashley Wilkes, who was the real love of Scarlet's life. Catherine knew it wouldn't be much trouble doing a love scene with him, either. Catherine had all the charm, the extreme beauty, the grace and the knowledge of what antebellum life was like. After all, she was a true Southerner. The movie was a huge hit. It set box office records that stood for almost 60 years. It was a monumental work, and often called the best movie ever made. No wonder that the upcoming actress Catherine Campbell wanted the part of Scarlet so badly. Of course, she didn't get it. She came awfully close though. Selznick said it was down to the wire between Catherine and Vivian. But, it was not to be for the hopeful Miss Campbell. Vivian Leigh got the part and went into the history books as Scarlet O'Hara. But Catherine didn't do too badly in the end. She got married not too long after that and gave up acting in order to take care of her husband and his mansion and the dozens of other duties that a world class socialite has to do. ***It's a Little Known Fact*** that the woman who very nearly was Scarlet O'Hara most have probably never heard of, but her husband was well known: the publishing giant William Randolph Hurst!

A Town Named Gravesend

No one knows for sure where Deborah Dunch is buried, but an appropriate epitaph would have been what one official wrote about her: "She is a dangerous woman." No, she wasn't a criminal. She never held up a bank or robbed a stagecoach. But she was dangerous to the religious establishment of the time. Deborah was English by birth, and she came from a wealthy family with both political and religious connections, but also one that believed strongly in civil liberties and religious non-conformity. She married Henry Moody, a well-connected landholder who was later given a knighthood, and thus she became Dame Deborah, or Lady Deborah. But when her husband died in 1629, she was only 33 years old. Those were days of great religious turmoil in England, and Deborah was attracted to Anabaptism, which was a Protestant sect that rejected infant baptism in the belief that baptism should be administered only to adult believers.   She felt strongly about her beliefs, so strongly that when she was unable to live in the oppressive religious climate in England, she sailed for the Massachusetts Bay Colony.   She had heard of the great new world across the Atlantic where people were going by the thousands to escape religious persecution of Europe and were finding the freedom to worship the way they believed.   Well almost!   That wasn't exactly the way it was in America in those days.   Yes, people came here to practice their own beliefs, but as soon as they arrived, one of the first things they did was set up communities of like-minded people and immediately ban any beliefs other than their own.   Like the Pilgrims and the Puritans and of course the Dutch Reformed Church.   What Deborah found was basically more of what she'd just left in England: people who wouldn't tolerate others who believed as they did.   She wasn't going to travel 4000 miles and give up her entire life just to face the same thing she faced in England.   So, she decided to do something about it.   And she did. She founded a town called Gravesend.   And she went further. She actually got the Dutch East India company who controlled the land to give her a grant and a signed contract assuring anyone in Gravesend could worship any religion they choose, without fear of prosecution. It was a first! ***It's a Little Known Fact*** that in a country that now prides itself on freedom of religion, Gravesend was the first place that it could actually happen. By the way, Gravesend was the only permanent settlement in colonial America planned and directed solely by a woman. That made it two firsts! And what happened to Gravesend? Nothing! It's still there. The town's name has changed, but it is still there, and today it is called Brooklyn, New York!

The Girl Named Jane

She was born Jane Korbel in Prague, Czechoslovakia. From the start this young woman was destined for a life in the public eye, but first the family had to survive. Her father Joseph was a teacher and a diplomat in Czechoslovakia, but when the Nazis stormed their country, the Korbel family had to flee. The Korbels wound up in London and Jane was enrolled in a good Catholic school. Her father got a job at the Czech. Embassy in London. Little Jane was often given the job of wearing a traditional Czech. costume and presenting flowers to arriving dignitaries. She made quite an impression, and it made quite an impression on little Jane too. After the war, Joseph brought his family to America. He got a job teaching at the University of Denver. Life at the university was good. Jane continued her Catholic education and was able to converse everyday with the top scholars and leaders at the school. It was a good and comfortable life. But there were lessons to be learned, like when the Vietnam War came along. Jane's father was an ardent supporter of America's actions in the war. He had seen first hand what the results of letting armed aggression go unchecked did in Europe and he knew that the same would happen to the people of South Vietnam if they didn't receive help. But Jane's family lived on a college campus, and the general attitude at the university was against involvement. Jane watched her father being criticized by many, and she saw him stand up for what he believed. She learned lessons in both commitment and diplomacy. Jane married Joe, the grandson of the founder of the Chicago Tribune, and the nephew of Alicia Patterson, who founded Newsday. When she went to college, she studied under Zbigniew Brezenski, the one time National Security Advisor to President Jimmy Carter. So it was no wonder that Jane was destined for a life in the public eye. But even Jane didn't know how far life would take her. She had a few surprises along the way, however, like discovering in her 60's that she was really Jewish by birth, not Catholic, and that her name was not Jane, but Madeline. ***It's a Little Known Fact*** that the woman who was raised a Catholic and named Jane Korbel went on to marry Joe Albright and become the first woman Secretary of State...Madeline Albright.

She Didn't Want To Be Bald

It is amazing how many success stories start out with the line "they were poor." Some people say that being poor gave them the drive and ambition to make a huge success of themselves. Maybe so. But that wasn't the case here. She made a success of herself alright, and she became one of the richest women in the country. But she wasn't driven by the fact that she was poor, and she was very poor. She came from a family that was absolutely mired in poverty. About the only thing she aspired to was a good job as a cook or domestic help. She just couldn't see past that. That's what her mother was, so she just figured that's what she'd be. And she was right, at least partially. Her first job was as a cook and housekeeper for a drug store owner. Then one day something happened to change things. She started losing her hair and didn't know why. She didn't want to be bald, so she started experimenting on the side a bit. She used chemicals and potions made up from ingredients found on the shelves at her employer's drug store. She had some failures but kept at it, and finally she did come up with a potion that restored her hair. That's when things started to change. Her friends noticed her newly invigorated head of hair and they wanted to use her potion, so she made more and sold it to them. The word spread about the marvelous new potion and before long she was spending more time making and bottling hair lotion than cooking and cleaning for her boss. She was making more money at it, too, so she quit her job and went into the cosmetic business for herself. This was a fairly brave move for anyone. For a while she did well, but when she came up with her next idea, she became rich beyond her wildest dreams. She started using ordinary housewives as sales people. Most of them had the time and she knew that they needed the extra income. She enlisted thousands of women to show and sell her hair and facial products to women all over America. In the process she became one of the richest women in

America. This occurred in 1911! No, she wasn't Mary Kay! ***It's a Little Known Fact*** that the first woman to make millions in the cosmetic industry was Sarah Breedlove Walker. She was also America's first black woman millionaire!

Bette's Cure

It really wasn't a very good year for Bette Nesmith. 1951 had started rather badly. She was recently divorced, and along with her young son Michael, was starting life anew. Like many woman who divorced in the family conscience days after the second world war, she was struggling somewhat to say the least. There was good news and bad news on the horizon for Bette. She was starting a new job, which was good. But her job required her to learn to use an electric typewriter, which wasn't so good. At that time in history, electric typewriters were something of a nuisance to people who had originally learned to type on manual typewriters. In the old days, typists were taught to rest their fingers on a home row of keys. Since the manual typewriters took a bit of finger pressure to make the hammer bar fly up and hit the page to make a letter imprint, most typist were a bit heavy handed. That presented a problem to those who were learning to use the electric machines. The new fangled typewriters would jump up and make a letter on the page at just the slightest touch of a key. The mistakes were hard to erase, especially from the carbon copies. And mistakes were plentiful. What should have made typing easier and simpler was for many typist causing them to slow down. The new electric typewriters were having the reverse effect of what they should have been doing! But Bette was a resourceful woman and she came up with a solution. It was to put white water based nail polish on the page to cover the errors. That did the trick! If she made an error in typing, rather than having to start over, she would simply paint over her error and go. Soon Bette moved to another secretarial job and her little trick of applying the white nail polish went with her. Quickly, it was noticed by other secretaries who wanted some for themselves. Then the idea hit her. She contacted a friend at an office supply store, and with their help started producing her little bottles of "Mistake Out!" That's what it was called at first. Her office supply friends suggested that she change the name and market more broadly. So she did. She changed the name and started to experiment with the formula until she came up with what millions of secretaries and people all over the world now know as "Liquid Paper." In 1957 she took the idea to IBM, but they rejected it. Undaunted, she continued to turn out Liquid Paper. Eventually she moved the company to Dallas, and in 1979 sold the company to Gillette for $48 million. It was another American success story of a cottage industry operating out of a kitchen, growing to an international company. Bette Nesmith died in 1980 at the young age of 56 years old, leaving about $50 million. Half went to Philanthropic Foundations and half to her son Michael. *It's a Little Known Fact* that the boy who inherited millions really didn't need it. He was already a huge success himself. Michael Nesmith is known from another period in our history, and another story -he became a member of the fantastically successful musical group The Monkeys!

And yes, her son Mike was a member of the Monkees, a 1960s TV show.

Nancy Green

Ouch! It was a horrible sound. First the squeal of automobile brakes and then a muffled thump and somebody falling to the ground. Several people ran over to see if they could help the elderly lady lying in the street, but it was too late. Nancy Green was dead. The strange thing was, though, that most of the people in the crowd recognized her. They didn't know her name, but they recognized her. The same thing happened at the hospital and then at the funeral home. Whenever someone looked at the face of the old woman, they were positive that, somehow, they knew who she was. Nancy Green was born in Kentucky. As a little girl, the thing she loved the most was watching her mama cook. She quickly picked up all of her mama's techniques and became quite a good cook herself. She moved from Kentucky to Chicago and that's where she met mister Christopher Rutt, a newspaperman. Chris was very excited because he had just found a new product that he was sure would take-off and make him a million dollars in no time at all. One thing he needed was somebody to represent him and show people how good the new product was. So he hired Nancy Green. Nancy would demonstrate his product to the visitors at the 1893 World's Fair in Chicago. Nancy was a hit. She not only had a genuine skill for cooking, but her warm and appealing personality made her presentation the most popular booth at the fair. Hundreds of people would gather around her booth just to watch Nancy prepare the new product. Why, they even had to hire police to keep the crowds moving. The fair officials ended up awarding her a medal for her showmanship. Chris Rutt was a happy man. He received over 50,000 orders from Nancy Green's presentation alone. She was so good that he gave her a lifetime contract. She went on to represent him for the next thirty years. The product she demonstrated at the fair did take off, just as Chris hoped it would. Nancy Green traveled the entire country for years introducing millions of people to this new idea that soon became one of America's most popular foods. ***It is a Little Known Fact*** that the 89-year old Nancy Green, who was born a slave and was killed by a car on the south side of Chicago had been for 30-years Aunt Jemima.

The Pitcher

It actually made some people mad when he broke the record, but break it he did. Hank Aaron hit more home runs than anyone else in history. For many years that honor was held by the great Babe Ruth. But now another great ball player had taken the title. And he did it honestly, the real way. Year after year, game after game, Hank Aaron stepped up to the plate and did his level best. His best was more than good enough. In addition to being the home run champ of the world, he also had more runs batted in, more total bases, and more extra base hits than anyone. So it was with good cause that Hank stepped up to the plate that day with tremendous pride. He was considered one of the most complete ballplayers around. But this day was a little different. Hank was seemingly unsure of himself this day, and with good cause. On the mound was the pitcher, a dreaded pitcher. This pitcher threw smoke, with fastballs clocked at over 110 miles an hour, and rarely walked anyone. This pitcher had a curve ball that could swing out over 8 feet and come back to the catchers glove with pin point accuracy. This was a pitcher who had once frustrated the great Ted Williams so badly that after striking out, Williams flung his bat down in disgust. Ted Williams, probably the greatest hitter in the history of baseball, reduced to throwing a bat around like a bush leaguer. And not just once, either. When Williams had his turn against the pitcher, he batted for 15 straight minutes and never touched the ball. Williams never got a hit off this pitcher in his entire career, striking out six consecutive times! No pitcher had ever done that to the great Ted Williams. Now it was Hammerin' Hank's turn. Pride made Hank determined to do what Williams couldn't, the same pride that enabled Hank to average over 30 home runs a season and to drive in 100 runs a record 13 straight seasons. As Hank stepped into the batter's box, he got a good look at the first pitch, a sinking fastball. He could see it was a strike, all right, but he swung and missed. The second pitch was a fastball, too. Hank swung and missed. Now fans were rising to their feet. It was clear that this was a monumental bat. As the pitcher wound up, a glimmer of Hank's determination seemed visible in his face. The pitch was another fastball. He swung just to make contact, but he missed. Strike three, Hank was out! Hank quietly turned and walked back to the dugout. He had met the same fate that Williams had at the hands of the pitcher.

It's a Little Known Fact that no man has ever stuck out both Ted Williams and Hank Aaron, but a woman sure did …famed softball pitcher Joan Joyce.

Dr. Ruth

Most people do not know the name Ruth Benerito, but come in contact with her product almost more than any other in their life. According to government statistics, 53% of people are touching one of her products right now. It all started back in the early 1930's when a company called Dupont invented a new product. It was called Nylon. When it hit the market place, it hit big. Nylon was light, strong as nails, looked good and was cheap to make. Needless to say, Dupont was pleased over the invention. Nylon was starting to take over everything, from parachutes to clothes to drapes to what women wore on their legs. But another industry took a big hit, and not a good one. That was the cotton industry. Cotton sales began to slump badly, and that didn't just affect one company. It affected millions of people. Thousands of Southern cotton farmers suddenly had no place to sell their crop. Textile workers were suddenly being laid-off, and not just in the South. Northern dye makers, shirt manufacturers, and trucking and shipping companies were also badly affected. When that many people are in trouble, the government steps in, and normally they just seem to make things worse. But not this time! The Department of Agriculture put their top people to work on the problem. They knew they had to find a way to make cotton an attractive and desired product once again. They did lots of things, like get famous designers to come up with fabulous new clothes and new colors, which is when the pastels became popular. They also started experimenting with lots of new kinds of products in an effort to come up with new cotton products. But none of that really worked very well. Ruth Benerito, who was a scientist for the USDA at the time, finally realized that what was needed was a different kind of cotton. She set about changing the actual nature of cotton itself, and changing nature is no easy job. It took her over 10 long years to do it. But she did! She is the one person who came up with what the American consumer was looking for all along: a natural fiber with a bonus. ***It's a Little Known Fact*** that this very creative and intelligent woman of science and holder of over 50 patents deserves the thanks of millions of now employed people and a very healthy cotton industry. The product she invented which literally changed an industry and a way of living was her development of no-iron cotton.

Ivan's Rescuer

Well, that was it! He knew that someday he'd go too far and he'd finally done it. Ivan had swam out in the lagoon to play with his friend Suzy and he'd gone too far, way too far. He had swam completely out of the safety of the lagoon and was far out in open water. He was exhausted from swimming. He called for help, but as he did, he was suddenly overwhelmed by a huge wave. Again he called for help, but it was becoming very clear that he wasn't going to make it back to shore. He was about to die. His last thoughts were of his family and friends that he knew he would never see again. He thought of the goals he had in his life, the ones he had accomplished and the many he had not. Ivan Tors was a movie and television producer. He was in the middle of a fairly big project when all this happened. It was on a break from production that he decided to take a pleasant swim in the lagoon with his friend Suzy. But Suzy was a much stronger swimmer than Ivan, and soon she was out of sight. When he finally realized that he was never going to catch up with her and she wasn't turning back, it was too late. He was too far and the water outside the lagoon was getting rough. He knew he couldn't make it back. He was finished. One thing that he found very sad was the fact that he wouldn't get to see Suzy any longer. They were becoming good friends. Ivan was going down for the last time when suddenly he felt something! It was Suzy. She had heard his cries for help and had returned. He felt her slide up next to him, and with nearly his last breath he sensed that he needed to hang on. His instinct told him to grab on for all he was worth, but he had just enough sense left to realize that might also prevent Suzy from swimming, too. He could feel her strength as she pulled him to the surface, held him up and carefully dragged him to shore. He felt the sand beneath his feet and realized that he was going to make it. He had been sure he wouldn't make it. And he wouldn't have if it hadn't been for Suzy. He thanked her in the only way he could. Since he was a television producer, he made her a television star. ***It's a Little Known Fact*** that producer Ivan Tors was saved from drowning by a future star, although Suzy had to impersonate a male to get the job. Suzy was television's Flipper!

The Man She Loved

Sarah had an age-old problem: her parents didn't approve of the man she loved. Tom was ten years older than Sarah, and was a bit rough at the edges. But Tom still came courting, and they were head over heels for each other. Things were slower back then. Courtships were longer, so it was a long time before Sarah realized her parents would never give their consent for her to marry Tom. As much as they loved each other, it looked like the relationship was doomed. Sarah's parents wouldn't consent, and Sarah was not willing to go against her parent's strong will. Tom said goodbye and left town when he realized he was never going to have the woman he loved. Some years later, Sarah heard that Tom had married someone else, and so did she. It is funny how things happen: her parents gave their approval of the man she finally married, but he turned out to be a no-account who was always in debt and could never keep a job. Sarah was miserable. She and her husband had three children. Sarah named one of the boys Tom. Every now and then she'd hear word of Tom. He and his wife had moved out of state and had a family of their own. Sarah often wished she'd gone against her parents and married Tom. But times were hard and she was too busy trying to keep her children fed to think about it much. And if things weren't hard enough, Sarah's husband died unexpectedly and left her penniless and deep in debt. Sarah was pretty low at that point. But her life was about to change. A few months later she answered a knock at her door, and there stood Tom. His wife had died also, and as soon as word reached him that Sarah was a widow, he came just as fast as he could. They fell into each other's arms. They did waste any time. They married, packed up Sarah's children and traveled to Tom's home. When Sarah got there, she discovered that Tom had two children of his own, a boy and a girl. The girl was named Sarah! That made her weep and love Tom all the more. His second child was a son, a tall, lanky boy that Sarah came to love and treat as her own. She taught him to read and nurtured his ambitions, and that boy's ambitions took him a long way, a very long way. ***It's a Little Known Fact*** that this was the true love story of Tom and Sarah Lincoln, parents of Abraham.

Cockeyed Charlie

They called him Cockeyed Charlie Parkhurst. He got his name from a patch he wore over one eye, but it never seem to bother him. Charlie was a stagecoach driver for Wells Fargo. He had the run from San Jose to Santa Cruz, California. Charlie was known as one of the best stagecoach drivers around. He was known to bring in coach and cargo on time, every time, sometimes covering as much as 60 miles a day. He was a fairly rough character. He played poker with the best of them, was known to have a drink or two, and even got in a few fights here and there. In the 1840's and 50's, he was well known by passenger and bandit alike. Even the bandits who laid in wait for the passing stagecoaches to rob them thought twice about it when they saw that Charlie was driving. Once he was stopped by a couple of no good highwaymen and the bandits took their eyes off Charley for one second when a woman passenger stumbled getting out of the stage.   Charlie grabbed his bull whip and with lightening speed clipped both of their guns right out of their hands. He was known for stopping many a-hold-up. Charlie voted in the first Presidential election held in California. He later said it was a proud moment in his life. No one knew just how proud until a few years later.   These things are known about Charlie today because he confided in a friend of his: a writer by the name of Bret Hart, who wrote it all down. But there was one more chapter in Charlie's life yet to be written, after his death at 67 years old. Charlie was found dead one day in his cabin. Nobody was sure what he died of, so they decided to do an autopsy. That's when they discovered a really big secret. Charlie was a woman. He, or she, had been disguising herself as a man for 50 years. That's the real reason we remember Charlie today, because she was the first to do something really big. *It's a Little Known Fact* that Cockeyed Charlie Parkhurst voted in a Presidential election 65 years before women got the right to vote.

So hats off to Cockeyed Charlie, the first woman in America to ever cast a vote!

She Just Couldn't Do It

Martha was not impressed. It wasn't going to happen and that's all there was to it. Her son knew better than to try and force the issue. He'd learned years ago that when Momma said she wasn't going to do something, then she wasn't going to do it. End of story, no use in discussing it. Most everyone else in the world thought it to be a great honor, but not Martha. She was something of a simple yet regal lady from the Midwest. She had spent the better part of her 70 years married to a farmer and raising children, who all became farmers too. And that included her son, who was a successful farmer himself for more than a dozen years. But that was before he lost his mind, that is. That's what Martha used to say about what her boy did: he lost his mind. What other reason could there be for quitting farming and doing what he did now? Back home, Martha was known as a good woman, excellent mother, good cook, and as loving and giving as anyone. She did have one little thing that kind of stuck out about her. She was still rather cranky about the outcome of the Civil War. Or for those from the South, the war between the states. Martha was a Southern sympathizer. She really admired the slower, easier, and in her mind, more gentile way of the old South. Now, most people don't see it that way, but there were many folks who did, some even today. She wasn't a proponent of slavery. She really didn't think anyone should own another person, and she raised her children to think that way too. But she thought there were probably better ways to do away with slavery than fighting a war. What really bothered her was the way the people of the South were treated by the Yankee invaders after the war ended. Carpetbaggers! They were everywhere. Thieves, cut-throats and robber barons descended on the what was left of the South and pretty much ravaged the land and the people. They took property, farms, plantations and equipment. Sometimes they did it through crooked government appointed officials, and sometimes they just stole it.

They even took what little dignity the people had left. They were a defeated people left to the ravages of unscrupulous men, and there was one man to blame for all of that. It was the criminal up in Washington D.C. Yes, she meant President Abraham Lincoln. She really thought that he should have stopped what was going on in the South. They had lost the war, but now, even what little they had left was being taken away by the worst of humankind. It was criminal. It was unforgivable. And now nearly 100 years later, Martha was not going to have it! When she was invited to the White House for a visit and it was suggested that she sleep in the Lincoln Bedroom, she adamantly refused. She'd rather sleep on the cold hard floor. And it was cold, for it was January. But that would be preferable to sleeping in the bed of a criminal. Most people consider it to be a great honor to be invited to sleep in the Lincoln Bedroom, but not Martha. And she didn't. *It's Little Known Fact* that Martha Young is only person in the 20th century who ever refused one of the most prestigious honors of all time, to sleep in the

Lincoln Bedroom. She did refuse, and she didn't much care that her son Harry S. Truman had just been elected President of the United States either!

Rosie The Riveter

Most people over the age of 40 have heard of Rosie the Riveter. Rosie wasn't just one woman, but about 5 million. It was during World War II when most of the able bodied men in the country went off to either Europe or the South Pacific to fight the war. Since the men were gone, the women of America stepped up! They filled the jobs that were vacated by the men, and they did the job just a well. Sometimes better! One famous world leader at a conference raised his glass in a toast and said, "Here's to the women of America and their unbelievable production, for without them the war would be lost." That was Joesph Stalin, and he wasn't the only one. Churchill said it too, so did DeGaulle, and many others. Even Herman Guering once told Hitler that he was astounded that American women would go to the factories in droves. For the most part German women didn't do that. They stayed home for most of the war. So did Japanese women. They all got active when the end was near, but the American women were there from the start. Many do not know that there actually was a Rosie the Riveter, two of them in fact. One was an aircraft worker named Rosina B. Bonavita, who inserted 3,345 rivets on the wing of a Grumman Avenger in just six hours! Has any man ever done that? And there was Rose Monroe, the woman who's picture became famous wearing the polka-dot bandanna wrapped around her head and the determined look on her face. That poster symbolized the will of the American working woman. There was one woman who was working in her third war. It was Mrs. Longstreet, who was the widow of the great Confederate General James Longstreet. At the age of eighty, Mrs. Longstreet worked at the Bell Aircraft factory in Marietta, Georgia. One who spent much of her young life going from orphanage to orphanage, she never understood why exactly, because she had a mother. But her mother that was mentally ill. She too worked as a riveter in an aircraft factory in Bakersfield, California.

One day the pretty young brunette was spotted by a photographer taking pictures for a moral building campaign by the government. She was very photogenic to say the least, that picture not only launched a thousand dreams for a thousand soldiers and sailors fighting around the world, but also started new career for the pretty aircraft worker. Most do not know that her first exposer came as a factory worker, but it did. ***It's a Little Known Fact*** that one of the real Rosie the Riveters and later one of the most famous stars of the silver screen was the very beautiful Marilyn Monroe.

Chaz Allen

Re-incarnation

She didn't talk about it very much because most people would look at her like she was crazy. But on the occasion she would open up to a few select friends and tell them about her past, as she did one night to Truman Capote. Truman was a well known author. He wrote multi-million selling books such as "In Cold Blood" and a few others. But he was also known as a confidant, especially of famous women. That was certainly the case here. She was a star of enormous scope, in movies, on stage, and recording. She had sold millions and millions of records in her life, and had done hundreds of interviews, but this was part of her secret. And maybe, her secret past. What was it? Well, she told friends that she once was an Abysserian Queen. And in another life, a Princess. Yes, she believe in re-incarnation. She knew that most people did not, and that many thought that she was crazy for expressing her beliefs. So she was quiet about them. But she did tell George Plimpton about being at the Crucifixion of Jesus. She said she remembered it very well and could spend hours describing that day in vivid detail. She told others about being a prostitute in Jerusalem and a slave in Ancient Egypt. She would talk for hours to her staff about being the wife of a merchant in Babylon and one of the prominent actors of the Renaissance. She was convinced that she had lived before, many times in many places. And she also knew that people didn't think much of her saying so. So she kept quiet. Was she a re-incarnation of many people in many lives now pasted into history? She believed it. In her final years she suffered with quite a bit of illness, both physical and mental. But even in her youth and at the height of her popularity, show business circles gossiped about the woman with a strange way of looking at the world. In the end, some say it went over the edge. But, she had one last song to sing. It was years after she had retired into seclusion from the public eye. One more multi-million seller. It is remembered for the unusual and mystifying lyrics. But more, people remember the way she sang that last song, a song that told the world that it was indeed her swan song. ***It's a Little Known Fact*** that singer and actress Peggy Lee had one more song to sing: the haunting "Is That All There Is?" The reason so many were caught up in her delivery of the strange little tune? Because she believed it herself.

The Demon Inside

Headstrong! That was the word to describe Amy Moore. At least that's what her husband David said. According to her parents, Amy had always been that way. Even as a child she would fixate on a particular thing and stay with it until she wore it out. That's pretty much how things finally ended up for Amy. Amy's husband David was actually her second husband. Her first was Dr. Charles Gloyd. Amy was a fair young maid of nineteen when Dr. Gloyd first came to her door. He was a dashing young man with an outstanding career in medicine ahead of him. An Army officer in the Civil War, Dr. Gloyd was recently discharged and was looking to set up practice in Belton, Missouri and needed a place to live. Hotel rooms were in short supply and what was available was expensive. He asked Amy's parents if he could rent a room. Yes, he could! It didn't take long before he was attracting the attention of young Amy. There was one problem however: the doctor seemed to have a drinking problem. He drank everyday, almost all day. Amy believed that the drinking was a result of the war and would stop when they got married. It did not. After the wedding, it got worse. Amy got pregnant and the drinking continued. The doctor became abusive and often wouldn't come home for days on end. Finally Amy could take it no more. Her father came to get her and the baby and rescue her from her alcoholic husband. But she didn't forget that experience. Not at all! Amy was bitter, very bitter. In her mind, all her dreams and hopes and plans of a good life with a loving and attentive husband and father to her child were now lost to demon alcohol. Amy eventually remarried, but she was still so bitter about what alcohol had done to her that she went on a campaign to end it forever. Her hard-headedness caused her to lose her second marriage. Her second husband David could not get used to her constant unending harping about alcohol. So one day when she was far away on a campaign, David divorced her. She had lost both marriages, and she never got over it! ***It's a Little Known Fact*** that because of her loss and hurt from what she deemed "demon drink", she took her seldom used first name Carrie and her husbands last name, Nation, and became known world wide for destroying saloons with her hatchet. She was the feisty Carrie Nation.

The Real Problem

During the turbulent 1960's, the people of America were divided on several issues. One of course was American involvement in Vietnam. Some newscasters and political commentators have tried to imply that it was the single issue that almost divided the country, at least ideologically. But nothing could be further from the truth. The truth is that several events were going on all at the same time which contributed to the unrest that happened. Not only Vietnam, but new attitudes were developing all over the place. There was a new kind of teenager, called a 'hippie', some called 'Flower children.' There was an anti-establishment backlash for a while against any big business. Now these people have grown up and are running a bunch of the big businesses. But ideology can cause some real problems. As much press as the hippie got protesting the war in Vietnam, over 3 million young men and women volunteered and went over to the Asian country to try and help an oppressed people. But we never hear much good about that in the media, and that was certainly not the first time for any of it. Another time it happened was in 1919. This time it was the women of America that wanted more say-so in things. They started banding together and marching, protesting at rallies and petitioning the political leaders of the day for what was then called Women's Suffrage. They wanted the vote, they wanted better pay, and who could blame them? One of the biggest obstacles at the time to their movement was the White House. Woodrow Wilson was President and it seemed that every piece of legislation favorable to Women's Suffrage that made it through Congress and reached the Oval Office was either rejected or just ignored for weeks on end with no action. It was a real frustration to the women and the few men working so hard to get suffrage passed into law. Petition after petition was met with denial after denial. Most thought that the President was against the women's suffrage movement. But they were wrong. President

Wilson pretty much favored women's rights. Then what was the hold up? ***It's a Little Known Fact***, and only discovered after his death, that for a while, the President was desperately ill and unable to carry on his normal duties. Someone else was doing all of the President's duties for him. Someone who was adamantly opposed to women's rights and stopped any and all petitions and legislation from even getting to the President to begin with. Someone who had the power and access to do just that very thing. Who was this person? The vice-president? The chief of staff? No, none of these! It was in fact the First Lady, Edith Wilson, who was adamantly opposed to the women's suffrage moment and stopped it at the President's door at every opportunity.

Princess

There's no question, for she was definitely a beautiful woman. She had already made a name for herself among beautiful people. Coming from somewhat humble roots, her beauty had in fact helped establish her career. It was her beauty which enchanted the charming prince from Monaco. But the Prince was a Royal. She was a commoner, not just any commoner, but an American! The romance of the American girl and the dashing Monacan Prince caused a scandal. But he was smitten and didn't much care if it cause a scandal or not in his small principality. He didn't care where she was from. He couldn't take his eyes off her. She had spent a lot of time in Europe traveling with the jet set, so she knew his country well. She had gambled in his famous casino, where anybody who was anybody went to see and be seen. Eventually, of course, her marriage to the Prince and her entry into the Royal Family would maker her even more of an international superstar, well known in social circles around the globe. But at this moment no one could see into the future, and it was unclear how their romance would turn out. Both families were wary of this possible union, and when the Prince admitted to his royal parents that he was considering proposing to the young American, they didn't know what to say. They could see what attracted him: her phenomenal beauty. And she was a Roman Catholic, which was quite important to them as well. He did the right thing: he met her parents, and they saw that he genuinely loved their daughter. He charmed her family the way he charmed her. They had to admit that a girl could do worse than marrying a Prince from Monte Carlo. Then, just as the Prince was getting ready to tell his parents that he would marry the girl no matter what, they approved of his choice. The couple married in an elaborate and breathtaking ceremony, and soon heir marriage was the talk of Europe. Her renowned beauty attracted artists from throughout Europe, and ballet, opera, and symphonic music flourished in Monaco as never before. It was almost as if this little country was in a state of grace, but not quite! No, not this time. ***It's a Little Known Fact*** that this American girl who captured a prince's heart became known around the world as Princess Alice. Alice Heine of New Orleans, who married Monaco's Prince Albert in 1890. Later a girl from Philadelphia named Grace also married a prince from Monaco. But Princess Anne was the first.

Chaz Allen

The Kaiser

World War I was called the war to end all wars. More than 25 nations slugged it out in battles all over Europe, the Middle East and North Africa. A total of 65 million soldiers fought in that war, 21 million of them were wounded and nearly 9 million killed. Historians have spent years trying to figure out what the war was all about, and many of them point straight to the emperor of Germany, Kaiser Wilhelm the Second, as the culprit who engineered the whole thing. Wilhelm was the grandson of William the First of Germany and of Britain's Queen Victoria. He was well known to have a tendency to talk too much. To put it bluntly, he just couldn't keep his mouth shut. He seemed to know nothing about tact and diplomacy. London newspapers loved to repeat his outbursts. When they reported him saying that the German people just didn't like the British, the ill will between the two countries shot up overnight.

Early on in his reign, world leaders criticized the Kaiser for all the muscle he seemed to be flexing. Some say that Wilhelm didn't really want war, but he didn't seem to mind the idea if it would help him reach his most prized goal: to turn Germany into a great empire, a country to be reckoned with. In the early 1900's, the Kaiser stretched British nerves to the breaking point when he started building German battleships. The powers around him could only imagine one purpose for all the war ships. England was so nervous that it made alliances with Russia and its old arch enemy France. And the rest is history. When the heir to the Austro-Hungarian throne was assassinated in 1914, war had come to Europe.

America finally took up arms in World War I when German submarines began attacking any ship in the Atlantic and sunk the Lusitania, which just happened to be carrying U.S. citizens. That was in 1917, and by 1918 the Treaty of Versailles was signed and the Great War was over. Wilhelm was forced to abdicate and when the peace treaty demanded that he be tried for promoting the war, he fled to Holland and sanctuary. Old Wilhelm lived just long enough to see Germany rise again during the Second World War. But there's a bit more to this story. One of his more impetuous acts made him famous when he was still Prince. It seems Buffalo Bill Cody had brought his Wild West show to Berlin and Wilhelm had a front-row seat. But the prince couldn't stand to sit on the sidelines, and so when one of the troupe's young performers got up to show off a rare shooting skill, he issued a challenge, daring the young marksman to shoot the very cigarette he was smoking from his mouth. The shooter accepted the challenge. Wilhelm put the cigarette in its holder, then clenched it in his teeth. The marksman stepped back 30 paces and took aim. Well, the shot was made and Wilhelm lived to tell about it. But later, the shooter wondered if a chance might have been missed to do the world a favor. "If my aim had been poorer," the wild west performer recalled, "I might have averted the Great War." ***It's a Little Known Fact*** that only one in a handful of sharp shooters could have made that shot and saved the Kaiser's hide, and this time the marksman happened to be a woman. And that would be, of course, America's very own Annie Oakley.

The Sound of Music

It still holds the record for the most people to ever see a movie. That's right! World wide it has been seen by more people than even "Gone with the Wind." Which movie is it? The huge 1964 hit and winner of 9 Academy awards: "The Sound of Music." A woman in England has seen this movie over 945 times, and that's in the theater. Now with her VHS, she has seen it hundreds more. For over 20 years it was the largest money grossing movie of all time. The only reason it isn't today is because of the increase of ticket prices. There are several memorable scenes, but one of the most memorable is the famous scene in the gazebo between Liesl and Rolf. Not only was it one of the best dance scene ever put down on film, but it was the quint-essential story of young love: two teenagers caught in the turbulence of a coming war. Liesl was played by the beautiful Charmian Carr and Rolf by the handsome Dan Truhitte, both Americans by the way.

In the movie industry, it often takes hours to set up lights, camera angles, sound, props and scenery, and it would really take its toll on the actors if they had to stand on the set for hours until it was ready. So it is common to hire local stand-ins for the actors. That way the crew can get the actual shots ready and then bring in the actors for the take. The stand-ins do earn their money. The stand-in for Charmian, or Liesl, was an attractive German girl named Gabriele. Gabriele was so attractive that she caught the eye of Dan Truhitte. Dan was charmed by the ravishing 17 year old and asked her out. She accepted and they started dating. It was a whirlwind romance, both on and off the movie set. When Dan saw Gabriele standing in for Liesl during the wedding scene in the mammoth cathedral, he couldn't resist any longer. He proposed marriage to the beautiful German that had captured his heart. Gabriele was a traditional girl, so her parent's permission was necessary. It was then that Dan got another surprise. ***It's a Little Known Fact*** that Dan Truhitte, who played Rolf, the romantic boyfriend to

Charmian Carr's Liesl, had to go and ask his fiancee's parents for Gabriele's hand in marriage. There he learned their real names were Rolf and Liesl!

Clumsy Norma

It may have been Christmas, but there was little joy in Norma's home that day. That was the day Fred, her alcoholic and unemployed father, decided to leave Norma's mother Peg and her two sisters to fend for themselves. Things seemed dire at the time for a woman left alone back in the early 1900s. There weren't many career opportunities, and the New Jersey winters were cold. But Peg was strong willed. She took in laundry to support her family. She was a good role model for her daughters, and at the age of 14, Norma took a modeling job to help out. Truth be told, Norma was a bit stage-struck. She was beautiful girl with dark brown hair and eyes, and it wasn't long before she was discovered and began a film career with Vita-Graph Studio. Her first appearance in film wasn't exactly a leading role—only the back of her head showed—but Norma worked hard, and within five years she had appeared in more than 100 films and increased her salary 10-fold. Vita-Graph got its money's worth out of Norma, and it was there that Norma learned the business inside and out. She not only played everything from a teenager to a grandma, she also assisted with costuming and make-up. Finally, Norma got her big break and was offered a contract out in Hollywood. Norma's chance to become a successful Hollywood actress was her mother Peg's chance to become the quintessential stage mother. By this time, the entire family was stage struck, including sisters Constance and Natalie. When Norma's film flopped and the studio shut down, it was Constance who got her another contract. Norma made good on that contract and starred in several films. But when the contract ran out, she decided to step out on her own. It was about the same time Norma fell in love and got married. And so it was that Norma and her new husband started their own production company. Again, Norma was a success. She became one of the glamorous Hollywood stars. But history will probably remember Norma more for being clumsy than glamorous, and starting one of Hollywood's biggest traditions. ***It's a Little Known Fact*** that at a gala grand opening of one of her films, young and lovely Norma Talmadge stumbled and fell into wet cement outside of Graumans Chinese Theatre, leaving the very first set of movie star's footprints.

Fine China

It seemed like from the time she was born, Josephine knew exactly what she wanted to be when she grew up. From as far back as she could remember she had a burning desire to live the life of a socialite. If this seems a somewhat shallow ambition, it wouldn't have mattered to Josephine. She married a merchant and politician named William Cochran, a man she was sure could support her in the fashion she was becoming accustom to, and she wanted to make sure it stayed that way. She even went so far as to change the spelling of her husband's last name. She added an "e" to the end of it to because she thought it looked "fancier." Josephine had a taste for all things fancy. She was given to extravagant entertaining. She had a houseful of servants and was living out her dreams. The fact that her husband was a populist, a man who believed in the virtues of the comman man, did not present a problem in Josephine's mind. And if it did so in

William's mind, he kept it to himself. As far as Josephine could see, the only real problem was that the servants kept chipping her good china when they washed the dishes. The loss of her china from clumsey servents bothered her so much that for a time Josephine washed her own dishes. Now she had a problem: she didn't trust her servants with her fine china, but the idea of washing her own dishes offended her. It just wasn't fitting for a woman in her position to wash her own dishes, she told her friends. Something had to be done. And if no one else was going to do it, she would. Josephine might have been a socialite, but she wasn't lazy or dumb. As it happened, William hadn't been feeling well and the couple had planned to go for a rest and let William recuperate. But Josephine was a woman with a mission and didn't feel in need of a rest, so she postponed her trip and sent William on without her. William soon returned home, feeling worse than before he left. And two weeks later he died. That's when she learned that all was not as rosey as she had thought. William made a lot of money, but the couple seemed to spend every dime he made. Josephine was left with just $1500 to her name, plus the huge debt she and William had accrued supporting her extravagant life style. She was without income and without a husband, but she still had that iron will she'd been born with. She set herself up in a shed out in back of her house and got to work. Within four years she went from socialite to mechanic and then to promoter as she began to advertise and sell the machine she developed. ***It's a Little Known Fact*** that it was Josephine Cochrane's one-time extravagant life of privilege that led to the world's first dishwashing machine, and what later became known as the Kitchen Aid division of the Whirlpool Corporation.

The Babysitter

It was a fairly lovely spring day, one that makes it feel good just to be alive. The temperature was hovering at about 75 degrees, trees were full and green, flowers were in full bloom, and the grass had been cut for the first time that season. It was a perfect day to go to the park if you lived in the city, which Betty did. She was the mother of two young children, one a toddler, a little girl, the other just an infant still in the bassinet. A pretty day like this was not to be missed. So Betty packed up her little ones and headed out the door. The day was everything that it promised to be. She set up a little blanket, got the baby out of the stroller, set out a few drinks and snacks and started enjoying her children and the day. Perfect! Before long a nice looking elderly woman came along and sat down on a park bench just a few yards away. The two women nodded a small greeting to each other. That's the way things went for about the next 15 minutes or so. Then trouble hit, the kind of trouble every parent watches for and probably fears the most. She had just taken the baby up in her arms to feed him, when the little girl wandered around behind her and disappeared out of sight for a few moments. Betty thought the child was right behind her, but it was hard for her to see with the baby in her lap. When she did turn around, she saw that the child had wondered quite a distance away and was headed straight for a busy city street. Betty screamed to the child to stop and come back, but the little one evidently didn't hear her mother screaming. Betty jumped up but suddenly realized that she had a baby in her arms, and she wasn't going to be able to get there in time carrying that infant. It was just then that the elderly woman noticed what was going on and told Betty to run, that she would watch the baby. Betty was tempted, but this was a complete stranger. Would the baby be fine, or was this a woman up to no good? The older woman again encouraged Betty to go after her little girl, and she must have seen the look of frustration on Betty's face because she said something that solved the dilemma, and Betty handed the baby to the woman on the bench and took off. What could that woman have said in those few seconds to make Betty feel so safe? ***It's a Little Known Fact*** that the elderly woman said something that identified her as a trustworthy person to almost anyone in America at that time. What was it? Well, she said: "Would it help dear if you knew that I am Walter Cronkite's mother?"

Chaz Allen

The Hypochondriac

We often remember what we want to remember! And that's especially true of famous people -our heros. We choose to remember their heroic feats and accomplishments, and that is probably the way it should be. After all most people don't do anything that changes the course of human events, so when someone does, it's good and right that they are remembered for their contribution to mankind. But often the part that is forgotten is every bit as interesting. Take the young woman who lay on her deathbed, her life hanging by a thread. She was waiting to die. She didn't die, but she became an invalid, captive to what may be the worst thing a person could have: psychoneurosis. Yes, she only believed she was sick. The doctors couldn't find a thing wrong with her, and they tried. But one thing the doctors did notice and that was virtually all of her illnesses followed family arguments. Her symptoms were real enough, and she was suffering. She had palpitations, shortness of breath, a racing heart beat and she was sick at the very site of food. If an unexpected or unwelcome visitor stopped by the house the symptoms grew worse. She would develop debilitating headaches and chest pains. It got so bad, she finally moved out of her family home and into her own place. That in itself was very unusual for a single women in those days. For the next three years things were different for her. She found she had limitless energy and willingly took on new responsibilities. She found herself caring for the sick and injured. Her sickness was a psychosis and she received no treatment for her own illness. Not much was known about it back then. After three short years she relapsed into her former state of imagined illnesses and waiting for death, though she lived for another 57 years. Why is this hypochondriac remembered today? Well, the three years that she was healthy and productive were during the Crimean War, and there she provided a service that gave women and the nursing profession respect world wide. ***It's a Little Known Fact*** that we have forgotten about the serious mental illness that she suffered from for most of her life, but we will always remember the three very loving and caring years in the life of Florence Nightingale.

A Grain of Rice

It was terrible! Daisy was discouraged to say the least. Just about all she could do was sit and feel sorry for herself and wonder how in the world she was going to function now. What a time for this to happen: on her wedding day of all days! Oh, she knew that other people had the condition though she really never paid much attention to it. She sure did now. Not to mention the pain! It happened as Daisy was leaving the church. The ceremony was beautiful, the groom handsome, and she thought she looked pretty good, too. She was a lovely radiant bride on her wedding day. Then as she and her new husband were leaving the church, a grain of rice suddenly lodged in her ear. Someone wasn't being very careful. Maybe a grain of rice in her ear was a minor inconvenience on a day such as this, but she needed to get it out. So Daisy went to a doctor to have it removed, but a horrible thing happened. While trying to remove the rice the doctor punctured her ear drum. That was bad alright, but it wasn't the worst news. Some years before as a child in her home town of Savannah, Georgia, Daisy lost the hearing of her other ear in an accident. Now she was nearly totally deaf! A pretty sad occurrence on her wedding day! Daisy was a rather talented actress, well known in New York, London, Paris, Berlin and other cities. How was she going to act now? How could she hear the other actors, the music, the directors? In 1886, there weren't a lot of resources for the deaf, and medical science didn't know much about it either. She decided to devote her life to her husband and moved to England, but unfortunately quickly became unhappy in her marriage. If she couldn't act on stage, then she decided to help where she could, and when the Spanish American war broke out, Daisy returned to America and organized a convalescent hospital for soldiers. After the war ended, she traveled once again to the British Isles. It was on one of her trips to Scotland where she saw large numbers of young girls working in factories instead of attending school. That would never do! Daisy knew she had found her calling. She returned to the United States with the idea of organizing young people to help make sure that didn't happen here. And she did! ***It's a Little Known Fact*** that the Juliette Daisy Low, the nearly totally deaf woman, gathered eighteen girls together on March 2, 1912, in an effort to keep American girls out of factories, and started something that has grown to be the world's largest voluntary organization for girls that has lasted over 90 years now: The Girl Scouts of America.

By Age Seven

She was just seven years old, and that is pretty young. Most seven year olds are in the first or second grade. They spend most of their school time learning the three R's, and they spend most of their free time playing with their friends or watching television. But that wasn't the case for this seven year old. Her life wasn't normal. Her father had been stricken with tuberculosis. He was in bad shape and really couldn't do much for himself. Hanging on to life was a full time job for Mr. Ash, and nothing else much mattered. In the 1940's, a person with consumption, as they used to call it, was certain to die. There was no cure. So all the little girl could do was make her father as comfortable as possible. Lulu, her mother, was forced to go to work. It wasn't easy, either. She looked for quite a while, and when she did find a job, it was twenty-five miles from home. That's twenty-five miles over rough roads in a car that was already twice past its expected life. Between the 10 hours a day at work and the drive back and forth, Lulu was gone from sun up to sun down. That left a little seven year old girl at home to care for an invalid father and to fend for herself. How many kids could have done it? Not many, for sure. When they needed groceries, or the father needed more medicine, or something broke and needed to be fixed, the only person that was there to do it was seven years old. She even had to travel all the way into the huge city of Houston on her own on many occasions to get clothes for herself because her mother couldn't get time off her job when the stores were open. Yes, this poor little girl had a tough road. But all the responsibility, determination, and dedication eventually paid off. A childhood like that will either make or break a person. A person who doesn't buckle under the pressure will learn how to take care of themselves and others. That's exactly what that little girl is known for today: caring for others, her dedication to God, and bringing a better life to millions of her fellow business partners and a fabulous array of products to the women of the world. ***It's a Little Known Fact*** that the little girl who had to care for an invalid father and even had to travel into Houston for clothes by herself at the tender age of seven grew up to be the world's leading manufacturer of women's cosmetics. She was responsible for starting more women in business than anyone else in history: the wonderfully irrepressible Mary Kay Ash.

Stagecoach May

How do you choose the path you walk in life? It is an age old question, and one that requires an individual answer from everyone. For one young man, it was a night in a blinding blizzard and the woman he owed his life to. Her name Stagecoach May. May was not like most women. She was born a slave in Tennessee. After the Civil War, she moved around with her family until she was full-grown. Full-grown she was: over six feet tall and weighing over 200 pounds. Most of it was muscle! She was something of an independent spirit. Not much was known much about her until she arrived in the Dakota territories, where she became a stagecoach driver. That is how she received the name "Stagecoach May." Someone once asked her what her last name was and she said, "I don't know that I have one. May has always been good enough." She carried a .38 Smith and Wesson, smoked 5 cigars a day, and was never known to back down from a fight. One of her regular freight runs was for the Blackfoot Indian Mission, located in a remote part of the territory. It was tough terrain and the trail had its share of dangers, but that really didn't bother May too much. It was on one of these runs in late fall that she took one of the local town boys along for a ride. That wasn't unusual, for she often took kids with her, usually just for the company. This youngster was special, and he seemed to idolize May. This day was different though. On the way to the mission, the weather turned rough. It started to snow, and then the wind started to blow hard. It was a blizzard, and May and the boy were forced to take cover. She built a quick make-shift shelter to protect them from the freezing wind and blowing snow. Everything looked like it would be alright until the wolves appeared. For most of the night, the wolves tried everything to get to the supplies on the wagon, and maybe to May and the boy, too. May wasn't going to have any of it. She shot several of them, and when the bullets ran out, she yelled, swung tree limbs and everything else she could to keep the wolves at bay. It worked! She saved the cargo and possibly their lives. Daylight brought a calm in the storm and help from the Blackfoot Indians, who were looking for them. It was an experience to remember, especially for the 8-year-old boy. He would remember May and her bravery all his life, and spoke about her often, even when he became a world renown celebrity. He was the most popular movie star in the country at one time. ***It's a Little Known Fact*** that a woman named Stagecoach May guided the life of this man more than anyone else. He often called her his idol. Not bad for a man who was idolized himself by millions. His name was …Gary Cooper!

From a Modest Home

Joseph and Ella were a very religious couple. As a matter of fact, Joseph was a Pentecostal preacher. And so it was in 1918 that they knelt down to pray with thankfulness when their fourth and final child, a beautiful baby girl, was born healthy and strong in their modest little home in Newport News, Virginia. Modest, because that's the kind of word people in Virginia used instead of "poor." But Joseph and Ella never told their children that they were poor, just that they were blessed. Every Sunday at church, all of Joseph's children would join in the singing and help out with the service. How happy Joseph was when that last little child turned out to be a fine singer. She was up on the altar singing and dancing at the age of three. Well, she might have been a big attraction on Sunday, but Ella knew it was just as important for her popular young daughter to be in school on Monday. She never stopped telling her children that education was the key to their escape from poverty. Well, that caused quite a complication in the family as the youngest girl kept getting more and more popular, and it looked like schooling was going to have to take a backseat to the opportunities that were coming her way. It was in Philadelphia that her career really began to take off. After years of singing in church, and for a few dollars here and there to make ends meet, she won an amateur singing contest and began working right away, singing in clubs and with some of the big bands back then. That was the good news. The bad news was that she would have to drop out of school. It was a hard decision but the young girl made a promise to herself that if she made something of her singing career, she would go back and try to make up for missing out on her education. Well she made quite a name for herself by singing on Broadway, in the movies and television. But she never forgot the promise she made to herself and her mother to go back and finish her education. *It's a Little Known Fact* that in 1985, the oldest graduate in the graduating class of Georgetown

University in Washington D.C. was that little girl, now 67 years old, going up to get her college diploma when they called out the name: Miss Pearl Bailey.

Quilt for All Seasons

Some people think quilting is old fashioned. Jan doesn't think so. She loves to quilt. She began quilting in 1991 and took to it very well. She took several quilting classes and even taught some quilting herself. Jan is also a designer who is an expert at cutaway applique'. She is so good at it, she was on T.V. teaching her pattern-making and demonstrating her fine applique work using freezer paper and needle-turning techniques. You might say Jan started quilting and never looked back. She took it with her everywhere. Why, you could see Jan with her cloth and needle and thread on an airplane, in a car, or at her hotel room, and you might think to yourself, "what a sweet old-fashioned girl." But this pretty blonde isn't as old-fashioned as her love for quilting might make her seem. Jan is a well-traveled woman. But if you're a quilter and want to make one of Jan's favorite designs, you should be careful with your choice of colors. When she designed 'Shooting Shuttles into Stars' for her Baltimore album quilt, she chose a light starry background fabric and a navy blue one for the four shuttles that make a circle on the block. Oh, you can go ahead and use those colors, but for the insignia design that is so delicately appliqued between them, do not use a yellow or gold color fabric. You see, since your cloth hasn't been to space you don't get to use gold. It seems the astronauts are given a silver insignia pin when they're picked for a shuttle mission, and you can use a silver gray color for yours. But when the astronauts get back from their first space flight they get a gold insignia pin to wear to show that they've been in orbit around the earth in the space shuttle. And that gold color is very special. Only people that have been in space get the privilege of wearing it. Each astronaut gets to carry a few personal items in a really small bag on each mission and Jan's quilting material got to fly into space. You might have a little more trouble getting your fabric into space than Jan did, though. How did Jan manage to use gold fabric for her quilts?

You see, Jan's fabric has flown on a shuttle mission. And she carried it! Jan really was well-traveled -she's been around the world over 400 times. ***It's a Little Known Fact*** that Jan Davis is one of NASA's space shuttle astronauts and one of America's foremost quilters!

Betty Boop Did It!

Rosie the Riveter -a name that referred to the wonderful, talented, hard working and dedicated women of America who stepped in an took over the jobs when the men went off to World war II. They took over the big jobs, jobs that many thought only a man could do: construction, building airplanes and battleships, and farming. The women of America proved there was almost no job that was exclusively for men. Women could do it all. And the country should be grateful, because the United States would never have won that awful war without them. That included the dedicated women who did their part to entertain America. One thing that has always been popular in America is the cartoon. Cartoons have been around as long as newspapers. A talented man named Disney can be thanked for bringing them to the movies. One very popular cartoon was Betty Boop. Cute little Betty was the original 20's flapper. She probably did more for liberating women than anyone, including Mae West. Betty Boop was the first cartoon to deal with femininity on a public scale. Betty's voice was done by the talented voice artist Mae Questel. Not only was she the voice of the famous Betty Boop, but she was also the voice of Olive Oyl, the skinny, neurotic girlfriend of Popeye the Sailor Man. Along with co-worker Jack Mercer, who did the voice of Popeye, she created a cartoon that was very popular with the fighting men overseas. Popeye was a great moral booster. He was good and kind, he loved Olive, and though he might have received a punch or two, he always beat the bad guy in the end. Not a bad venue for a bunch a guys fighting a war to see, and Popeye enjoys popularity to this very day. For about 3 years, Jack Mercer was off fighting the war. But the production of the good natured Popeye cartoons needed to go on for the entertainment and moral of the fighting men. ***It's a Little Known Fact*** that Rosie the Riveter stepped in here too. Mae Questel, the voice of Betty Boop and Olive Oyl, also did the voice of

Popeye while Jack was off at the war, and no one ever knew the difference.

Gold Fever

At one time there were some real boom and bust towns in this country. One day a town was loaded with hundreds, perhaps thousands of people and dozens of thriving businesses, and the next day it was practically a ghost town. There are two industries that have caused this situation in American history. One was the discovery of oil, but the big one, the one that caused the most boom and bust syndrome, was gold! When gold was discovered, every near-do-well who couldn't make a living scratching the ground or driving a herd would pack up and head for the promise land in the hopes of striking it rich. And a few did! Yes, there were a few who actually wound up fabulously wealthy. But the whole idea was fraught with danger. Not only was traveling a bit dangerous in those days, after reaching their destination, a person faced unbelievable odds. Good land was claimed quickly. Those who did make a claim were lucky if they weren't attacked by claim jumpers or robbed by highwaymen on the way to cash it in. Not to mention the physical work. Mining is hard work, especially back then. Even panning a few nuggets out of a stream was hard, back breaking work and it had to be done for hours just to get a few grains of the precious mineral. But the discovery of gold did make a few people quite rich. Very rich, indeed. Leadville, Colorado is a good example. Leadville was a major strike that gave up her gold for years. At one time the town was about as boom as it could get. People arrived from all over the country with a dream of becoming rich, and several did. Like Mrs. Sarah Ray. Yes, Mrs. Ray!. She became the first millionaire in Leadville. She made a million dollars at a time when a nickel would buy a gallon of milk. But she didn't do it by digging in the ground, or selling drinks to thirsty miners, or even feeding them. ***It's a Little Known Fact*** that the first Leadville millionaire, and one of the first women ever to make a million on her own, did it by taking in laundry.

The Recluse

It was getting to be ridiculous! Vinnie loved her sister and understood that she was a bit strange, and Vinnie was willing to help on the occasion. But this was ridiculous! That was exactly what was going through Vinnie's mind as she headed toward the dress maker again! She was going to be fitted for a dress. She really didn't mind being fitted for a new dress, and this was at a time when almost all dresses were hand made. The problem was that the dress wasn't for her! It was for her very reclusive sister, and it wasn't the first time, either. Vinnie had been doing it for some time. Vinnie's sister had a quite a few dresses and she had never been fitted for any of them. It would be a white dress. Vinnie knew that! Her sister had a whole closet of dresses and every one of them were white. It was the only color she would wear. Dresses, hat, gloves, shoes, petticoat, and blouses: all were white! It was a good thing that Vinnie was the exact same size as her sister, or this couldn't have been done at all. She even toyed with the idea of gaining a bit of weight so that she couldn't be the model any longer, but that wouldn't be the answer. And it didn't end with dresses either. Vinnie's sister was paranoid and excessively shy. Not too long before the visit to the dressmaker, Vinnie's sister took ill. She required a doctor's visit. She wouldn't go to the doctor's office, so Vinnie summoned the doctor to her sister's house. That didn't work out so well, either. Vinnie's sister wouldn't allow the doctor to examine her because she was too shy. The poor doctor had to do the entire examination, as best he could anyway, from another room. He wasn't even allowed to see his patient! Also, Vinnie had to address all of her sister's correspondence. Her sister wrote brilliant letters to friends, politicians and others, but she refused to address the envelopes because she was afraid that someone would discover her handwriting. Not only did she write brilliant letters, she also wrote a few other things, too. Her work is very familiar. ***It's a Little Known Fact*** that this total recluse who would never venture out of the her house, would wear only white, would only allow a doctor to examine her from another room, had her sister fitted for her dresses and write her envelopes, was also the woman who wrote some of the most brilliant pieces of poetry ever penned. Vinnie's sister was the very talented, but reclusive, Emily Dickinson.

The Champ

Heavy weight fighters have always attracted a crowd and big money. Today a championship match can gross over $100 million. The fighters themselves get twenty or thirty million just for one fight. That's a lot of money. But few are willing to do what those men do to make that money. Prize fighters make good money and usually become very famous. Take for example Joe Louis or Rocky Marciano or John L. Sullivan. It's been over 70 years since Sullivan fought, but most have heard his name. He was a bare-knuckles champion, meaning he didn't use gloves. Now talk about tough hombres! John was scheduled to fight a man by the name of Battlin' Jack one evening. The fight was well promoted and the men not only knew each other but were friends. Which is why what happened next is so interesting. Jack had a little daughter, Mary Jane, who was seven at the time. She knew her daddy worked at a boxing gym and even saw him spar a few times. On this night, Mary Jane begged to go to the match. Jack was against it but he couldn't find a baby sitter, so he agreed as long as Mary Jane agree to behave herself. He sat her in the front row and the fight began. Jack was pretty good, but no real match for the World Champion Sullivan. Jack was getting knocked around pretty good. When a cut opened over his eye and blood started running down his face, he worried about how this would affect little Mary Jane. He didn't have wonder long. She flew out of her seat in the middle of the fight, grabbed Sullivan's leg and started biting it. Sullivan was in shock and pain all at the same time. He didn't want to the hurt the child, but he didn't want to be bitten either. The referee and Mary Jane's father both tried to loosen her locked jaw, but her teeth were set. Finally, in frustration, Sullivan laid down on the canvas and pretended to be out cold. That did it! The child let go. ***It's a Little Known Fact*** that the world's bare knuckles Heavyweight Champ was taken down by a seven year old girl. And that's really surprising, for she became the world's model of feminine behavior a few years later. She was Battlin' Jack West's little daughter alright, and they just called her Mae West.

The Boarding House

It was just another fire, just another old run down boarding house, on just another street in old Ft. Worth. There was only one casualty, the owner Eunice Gray. Many people saw her on the street from time to time, and occasionally she would speak, but the for most part she kept to herself. She ran the boarding house and took care of the few paying guests she had, but that was about it. Nothing remarkable really. There was one gentleman who would come through from time to time and stay at the boarding house. Most people thought he was just another guest, maybe a traveling salesman saving a few bucks by staying at the boarding house rather than one of Ft. Worth's nicer hotels. But some on the street thought there was more to the relationship. The man's identity is not known for sure, but Eunice Gray's is. Eunice wasn't her real name, but considering her past, who could blame her for changing it? Prior to becoming a docile boarding house owner, she had spent some time in South America. But that was only because it was just too dangerous for her to remain in the United States. She was being sought after by every law enforcement agency in the country, including a few of the private services, like Pinkerton's. Eunice was actually the mastermind behind one of the most notorious outlaw gangs of the Old West. She was once a school teacher and housewife in Ft. Worth, when she met Harry. Harry was something of a wild one, and the young school teacher couldn't resist the temptation to follow along. But when she learned that Harry and his partner had robbed the Union Pacific Train outside of Tipton, Wyoming, and had only netted $50, she took control. For the next five years she made the plans, she choose the targets, she planned the robberies and she took care of the money. It was because of her planning and cunning, and not her notorious boyfriend and his partner, that their gang became one of the most successful and infamous of the West. It is not know what happened to Harry and his partner for sure, but who was that gentleman caller who showed up at the boarding house from time to time for years? And what became of Eunice, or Etta. That was her real name, Etta Place. A reporter for the Ft. Worth Press discovered her real identity in 1962. ***It's a Little Known Fact*** that the woman who died in the boarding house fire was the little known mastermind and leader of one of the most notorious outlaw gangs of the West, and the girlfriend of Harry Longbough, better known as The Sundance Kid, friend and partner of Butch Cassidy.

The Gripper

Most don't like to admit it, or even think about it much, but somewhere down our long line of ancestors, there was probably a barbarian or two. The truth is we didn't come into this world with a lot of social know-how. Historians usually mark the Middle Ages as the time when people first started to put on a good face in front of company. In the 13th century, for instance, teachers warned their charges that if they were the fourth or fifth person to gnaw on a bone, they'd best not put it back in the serving dish. In the 14th century, diners were cautioned not to pick their teeth with their dinner knives, and by the 1500's the rules of fine etiquette finally put a stop to all that nose blowing on the table cloth. We've sure had our ups and downs with what's considered correct in these more modern times. Why, not too long ago the rules for social behavior were so numerous and so complex that most people couldn't even hope to remember them. It seems we've inherited that list of do's and don'ts from the European aristocrats and a few Americans who've set themselves up as high society in charge of judging the rest of America. There was a time when books about etiquette implied that if you didn't belong to a certain social group, you were inferior, and lazy and smelly to boot. Some people believed this way of thinking to be crazy, and a real threat to what this country was all about. After all, that's what people working to improve themselves would try to become, forgetting about a society that believed all people were created equal. All of this made one newspaper woman so mad that she would rant and rave about it on a regular basis. In fact, she griped so much that a friend of hers dared her to do something about it. And so she did. ***It's a Little Known Fact*** that this one-time novelist wrote a book to protest and complain about the snobbish ideas concerning etiquette in America, and she found instead that she had introduced the cornerstone for a whole new way of thinking. To her, snobbery was the height of rudeness, and common sense and consideration of others the golden attributes of gracious behavior. And much to the surprise of Emily Post, most of America agreed with her.

Recipes

Grandmothers are always known for their cooking. Many of the best recipes have been either handed down through generations or discovered by trial and error. Many grandmothers measure ingredients as a dab of this, a dollop of that, a pinch of salt, a smidgen of clove, or a sprinkle of pepper. How big is a dollop? What measured a pinch? For the most part, that was how cooking and recipes were handed down for five thousand years. People wrote them down so they could remember what ingredients went into a dish, but it was always portioned out with a dollop, or a dash, or a dab! Then something happened that necessitated a change. One of the finest cooking schools in the world, the famed Boston Cooking School, was becoming so famous for its food that people started requesting that the school mail out their recipes. So they did. A dollop here, a dash there. But then complaints starting coming back that the food

297

didn't taste right. The recipes didn't live up to the reputation of the school. That's when one of the instructors at the famed Boston Cooking School, and also one of the finest cooks in the country, realized that the method of measurement had to be better controlled. So, she started rewriting all of the schools recipes, replacing a dab with 1/3 teaspoon, or a dollop with 1 oz. For the first time cooks all over the country could make the famed recipes in their own home to taste just like they did at the Boston Cooking School. They became so famous that the School assembled and sold the very first cookbook with exact measurements for adding ingredients. Every cookbook since has followed suit. No, this chef, didn't win a war, or get elected to public office or win the Nobel Peace Prize, but she affected more lives than all the politicians, generals and Nobel prize winners put together. She should be thanked for her fabulous recipes, and for her wonderful candy too. *It's a Little Known Fact* that the woman who made it possible for good cooks everywhere to receive the love and adulation of their families and diners is still remembered today for some of the best candy in the world. Her name was Fannie Farmer.

Chaz Allen

She Remembered

Gladys Louise Smith was a tiny thing! She was all grown up, but she was still a small person, even for a woman. As one man said, she looked so frail that you could knock her over with a feather. But, frail she was not! Like many people who achieve greatness, Gladys grew up poor. She once said she could remember as a child falling asleep at night huddled together with her sisters under one blanket to share body heat because there was no money for coal to heat the house. Even in the dead of a New York winter. She remembered how her mother struggled with five children and no husband, working two jobs to just make enough money to pay the rent and buy the most meager rations of food for six people. She remembered many days with no food at all. Gladys promised herself that she would remember those times when she grew up, and she did! The family was so desperate that Gladys started her first full time job at only eight years old. The only job she could find was in a theater acting as a child of the star of the play. But she was good. By the time she was 13, she was making more money than the rest of her family combined. As she grew older and started to make more money, she remembered the tough times. She started to help others who were in the same situation she was once in herself. When WW I broke out in Europe and the U.S. sent soldiers and sailors to fight, she was one of the first to go on the campaign trail and sell government bonds to pay for the war. She sold a lot of bonds. When the war was over she went to work establishing a special educational fund of scholarships for returning military men and women so they could get a free college education and better their lives. Gladys decided to leave the stage and go into the movies. Everyone told her it was a huge error. Flickers were a passing fad. She would starve again. But she had a feeling, so she went. And there in her new business, she was just as powerful. She was the very first to negociate salary and creative control for the actors on a movie. She was the first actor of any kind to make over $500 a week. At a time the average salary for an American was $500 a year! When a few negotiations didn't go the way she thought they should, she started and ran one of the largest movie companies in the world: famed United Artist. But Gladys isn't remembered for any of that. She is not remembered as the hard fighting, tough as nails negotiator that changed Hollywood and the movies forever, or as the woman who raised more money for war bonds than any other person in WWI. She isn't even remembered as the woman who started the very first educational funding for returning veterans. She is remembered as exactly the opposite. ***It's a Little Known Fact*** that this tiny woman, who was an absolute powerhouse of a business person and entrepreneur, is remembered as the timid, shy and very sweet vision of loveliness that sMary Pickford presented to the world.

About the Author

Chaz Allen is the writer/producer and creator of one of the most popular radio programs in America "Little Known Facts." The program is broadcast on over 475 stations and his stories are syndicated in over 150 newspapers. Chaz is an award winning television producer and national C.I.T.E. award winner.

Printed in the United States
17553LVS00001B/7-45